Signs of His Coming

The Season of the Return of Jesus Christ

DOUGLAS M. CHATHAM

Signs of His Coming

The Season of the Return of Jesus Christ

DOUGLAS M. CHATHAM

Mall Publishing Co.
THE PRINTED WORD THE PLANTED SEED
HIGHLAND PARK, ILLINOIS

In nomine Patris et Filii et Spiritus Sancti.

Printed in the United States of America
Published by:
Mall Publishing Company
641 Homewood Avenue
Highland Park, Illinois 60035
877.203.2453

Cover Design by Douglas Chatham Jr.
Text Layout Marlon B. Villadiego

ISBN: 1-934165-33-6

For licensing / copyright information, for additional copies or for use in specialized settings contact:

Douglas M. Chatham

6375 Seymour PL NW
Acworth, GA 30101-8063
Email: drchat1@bellsouth.net

INTRODUCTION for *Signs of His Coming*

I HAVE HAD the distinct honor of knowing Dr. Douglas Chatham for the past ten years. Over the course of time, our relationship has progressed from being a student in his classes at Beulah Heights University to now serving him as his pastor. Whether in the classroom or in the pulpit, Dr. Chatham graciously teaches and preaches the Word of God in such a way that the listener might always benefit. Spend even just a few minutes in his presence and it will become obvious that Dr. Chatham's knowledge of the Bible clearly comes from the Author.

In his significantly important and timely book, *Signs of His Coming*, Dr. Chatham presents what is a clear Biblical presentation of eschatology concerning the times in which we now live. While there are certainly varying views on this subject, I am confident that you will gain a much deeper appreciation for and a heightened expectation for the imminent return of Jesus Christ

Join me in the exciting journey of reading *Signs of His Coming*. The experience will surely fill your heart with joy as you discover, in greater measure, the certainty of our Lord's soon return. *Signs of His Coming* serves as a clarion call to the Body of Christ, and to the world, that Jesus is indeed coming back!

– Shell Osbon, Pastor, Smyrna, Georgia

PREFACE

FORTY-SIX YEARS LATER, I still remember seeing the words, "They live too low who live beneath the stars." I read the line from a placard mounted above my bus seat while traveling through a tunnel under the Detroit River, oddly enough. The idea intrigued me and the words stuck in my head. The sky is not the limit. Our destiny is beyond the stars. Our outlook is an "uplook!" We should be looking up, especially these days. "And there will be signs in the sun, in the moon, and in the stars…"[1] "Now when these things begin to happen, look up, and lift up your heads, because your redemption draws near."[2] If we are living without looking up, we are living too low.

This is a book intended to stir hope in your heart. The best is yet to be! The time in which we live is loaded with pessimism. Dreams die, dollars devalue, terrorism threatens and crime increases. Political pundits pontificate and prescribe new paths to prosperity; but a less confident and more cautious public deals with sobering new realities. Since the downturn of the United States and other major world economies, the security of many monetary "comfort zones" has been shattered. But this book points to the presence of a safe and permanent comfort zone, the blessed hope that is available to every believer in Christ. Now, more than ever, there is good reason to look beyond the limits of the present moment. As you read these pages, you will see the bigger picture of the threshold which we have crossed: an entrance into an awesome season of the signs of the Second Coming of the Lord Jesus Christ. The Second Coming empowers us with hope. The power of hope will shatter the sense of helplessness and shake us loose from the paralysis of despair.

Our situations are shaped by God to help us more earnestly desire the Day of Christ. Those who are sleeping safely on a soft pillow never desperately desire the dawn. Yet, think how many soldiers, entrenched on the battlegrounds of numerous wars, have shivered silently in the fearful dark and prayed for the first light of dawn to come! Consider how many storm-tossed sailors, through all the centuries of sea-faring, have clung to broken pieces of their ships through long sleepless nights and wished for daylight! Part of our preparation for the Second Coming is disenchantment with deceptive comforts. Out of the present stormy darkness, we pray fervently for the Day. According to ancient prophecy, the appearing again of the Lord Jesus Christ is at hand. For believers in this sin-darkened world, He is the Day Star that signals the dawn. The long dark night of man's inhumanity to man, and the rebellion of creation against Creator, is almost over. The Sun of Righteousness is about to appear.

Predictions of the end of this age abound, whether in prophecies recorded in ancient cultures or in the dire declarations of present-day psychics. Very few describe any thing that we might happily anticipate. Scenarios range from cosmic catastrophes such as comets colliding with Earth to a global nuclear war and a subsequent nuclear winter. This book offers a more appealing alternative: a delightful rediscovery of all the bright aspects of a wonderful future in the Kingdom of God. Our long winter of discontent and discouragement is ending, and the cosmic Spring of all Creation is coming. The coming of Jesus, who is The Dayspring, brings with Him the renewing of all things good and beautiful - the Messianic Age – followed by a glorious eternity. The season of His coming is marked by a spectacular season of prophetic fulfillments, and this book is a study of these fulfillments, or signs.

What about the number 666, the Antichrist, the Battle of Armageddon and the Millennial Temple? This book may not satisfy all curiosity concerning these questions. It will, however, provide a clear overview of major biblical prophecies relating to the Second Coming. Moreover, special attention will be given to everything comforting that Jesus has told us about Heaven and His coming. This book purposely avoids giving too much attention to the sensational topics currently in vogue at prophecy conferences. During a ministry spanning more than half a century, I have read hundreds of books relating to end-time prophecy. Various prophetic fads ran their course and faded away. One well-known writer said Armageddon would happen in 1982. A famous radio preacher was certain that the Second Coming would take place in September of 1988. Other prophecies centered around "Y2K," the year two thousand. Another fad that was embraced by many claimed that, according to an ancient Maya prophecy, the world would end on December 21, 2012. You will find that this book is neither about dates nor fads. It is about simply understanding what the Bible says about the last days of this age and especially about the signs of the season in which Jesus Christ will return. This book is not about timetables; it is about the times.

The theological level of the book is intentionally designed for youth, teen and college students whose minds are open. Perhaps it will serve to provide a worthy debate topic. It is a simple book, written largely in layman's language. My hope is that *Signs of His Coming* will serve as a useful tool for sharing your faith with other people by loaning it to them. You should find it a useful study book for your prayer or connection group. Perhaps you will find it suitable for mailing to a friend or family member as a means for the Holy Spirit to teach them and draw them to Jesus. Perhaps just reading this book will put some troubled mind to rest in the realization that God is on His throne, and He hasn't moved. He is well able to provide for us and to fight battles for us. This book will make you wise, able to discern the times, and thereby empower you to live not for this world only.

– Douglas M. Chatham

ENDNOTES FOR PREFACE

1. Luke 21:25a
2. Luke 21:28

Contents

Chapter One

A CONTEMPORARY PERSPECTIVE ON THE END OF THE AGE

When is Now?

A SMALL CHILD'S question still baffles adults: "When is *now*?" For the children's sake, we pretend that we know. "Why, *now* is… well, *now* is…it's right now – this present moment!" But of course, that's just another way of saying "now." It has been said that "now" is where two eternities meet: the past and the future. The past and the future are like two cosmic clockwork wheels, one working against the other. At the point on the circle of each where the cogs of the past mesh with the cogs of the future, is the moment that we call "now." But the wheels of past and future eternity never stop, so our "now" never stays. All of our "now" moments, when strung together over a lifetime, make up only one slightly longer "now." The reality of our natural existence, on the scale of eternity, is incredibly limited. Earthly life spans are spent by a process in which the future constantly changes into the past.

What is true about "now" for every human is also true of human history; and of the universe itself. Science tells us that the universe had a beginning. Looking backward in space time, there was a point in time when there was no time. Looking backward to the origin of space, there was a point when there was no space. There is a causal structure in space time. Science tells us that space is emergent.[1] The universe is not static; not eternal. It is gradually decaying. So, our "now" is passing away. There will be an end to chronological time, as we know it. Chronological time is a created thing. Our "now" is temporal. On the other hand, God exists in an eternal "now." He always was and always will be. He exists outside of what we understand as chronological time. Time was a temporary arrangement for humankind, which God set up on the fourth day of creation. The Bible tells of a time when time will end.

> Then the angel I had seen standing on the sea and on the land raised his right hand to heaven. And he swore by him who lives for ever and ever, who created the heavens and all that is in them, the earth and all that is in it, and the sea and all that is in it, and said, "There will be no more delay! But in the days when the seventh angel is about to sound his trumpet, the mystery of God will be accomplished, just as he announced to his servants the prophets."[2]

Ages ago, the Hebrew prophets peered down the corridor of the centuries and depicted details of the last days. These ancient seers described an epochal stage upon which would be enacted a series of events relating to the Day of the Lord. They interpreted all intervening time as a build-up to the ultimate end, when Yahweh would judge the earth. Jesus Christ taught that His Second Coming would be in the last days, and elaborated on events that would precede His Second Coming. The New Testament writers followed the pattern of the Old Testament prophets and saw the coming of Christ at the end of time, which is only being temporarily delayed to allow the preaching of the Gospel.

Back to the "now" problem! If time will end, what will happen to our temporal "now?" It will flee away, and we will have no time left to exist. Jesus Christ is our only hope beyond the present "now." In the eternal Godhead, He lives in an eternal "now." He always was and always will be. He has an eternal past and an eternal future. He is the eternal "I Am." He is the only real link between the two directions of infinity. He lives in, but transcends the moment we call "now." We can only live in the temporal "now" until we partake of the divine nature of Jesus. He came into our "now" from outside all sense of time. He came with a message of love from the God of Eternity who wants us to be eternal. The good news of the Gospel is that Jesus gives eternal life to those who receive Him.

What Next?

The world waits in wonderment for the curtain to go up on the next act. The suspense builds as each scene seems less scripted than the one before. The perfect storm is forming: massive market meltdowns, failed infrastructures, unwinnable wars, rogue nations with nukes, threats of terrorism attacks, and breakdown of borders. What next? A superpower government can't govern, and global village neighbors are nervous. Change has been called for, and so much change has come so quickly, that the general public feels like Rip Van Winkle, freshly awakened from a twenty-year nap.

The non-Christian has no way of correctly perceiving current events, and no valid vision of the future. History is certainly in the making, but what is it making? Who can say for sure? Who is worthy to open the book of the future? The answer is embedded in the Bible. In Revelation 5, we find that only Jesus Christ can open the seals and unroll the meaning of history. Secular historians like Durant and Toynbee do not have the key. Without Jesus Christ, secular history is, as Shakespeare's Macbeth puts it, only "a tale told by an idiot, full of sound and fury, signifying nothing." History is really His story, and without Him it has no plot. The good news is that history really does have a script. "Truth may seem forever on the scaffold and wrong forever on the throne, but behind the dim unknown standeth God within the shadow keeping watch above His own."[3] Scripture tells us in Romans 8:28 that all things work together for good, for us who love God and are called according to His purpose.

The one timeless book that never fails to be true has revealed what is yet to be. Its prophecies make known to us where present events will lead. The Lord of time and space is in charge of the future. He is our Lord. He is following a plan previously proclaimed by the prophets. Unbelievers grope in darkness as children of the night. Christians are children of the day and must not be confused by current circumstances. We exist each day on the edge of eternity, but we don't have to be on edge about it. Someone has said that if you can keep your head while others are losing theirs, you'll be a head taller than everyone else! In these times, we have a golden opportunity to demonstrate the definite difference made by the inner peace which passes all understanding. We live in the now; but we who have found Jesus, have found our future.

Eternity Is in Our Hearts

When Jesus returns to catch away all those who are spiritually united with Him, He will pull them out of this temporary "now" time frame, and take them into a realm where the past no longer devours the future. That is the true reality for which we were created. An indication of this is the fact that God has placed, deep within all our hearts, the haunting awareness that there is much more than this temporal life. At the very core of our being, we know that we belong in eternity. As the writer of Ecclesiastes tells us, "He has made everything beautiful in its time. He has also set eternity in the hearts of men; yet they cannot fathom what God has done from beginning to end."[4] We inwardly long for the very thing that God wants for us. We don't understand how eternity works – what God has done before and what He will do beyond – but we know that he wants to take us into a realm where there is no aging or death. We long for Jesus to come.

In *Tramp for the Lord,* Corrie ten Boom tells about speaking to a group of young Bible students about the Second Coming of Christ. A youthful seminarian challenged her, saying, "For two thousand years, Christians have believed this myth. Can't you understand all this talk is nonsense?" The elderly Dutch woman who had survived one of Hitler's death camps smiled and said, "Thank you, young man, for proving that Jesus is coming in this generation. The Bible says the generation who shall see His return shall hear scoffers such as you. You, my young friend, are one of the 'signs of the times.'"[5] She was right. In Peter's second epistle, we find the words, "...in the last days, scoffers will come...They will say, "Where is this 'coming' he promised?"[6] The book you now hold in your hands is about the signs of His coming. If this topic holds your interest, please be forewarned that for many others it does not. Society in general no longer pays much attention to prophecy. May you be so fortunate as to find others who share your interest!

Looking for His Appearing

The title on the cover of this book caught your eye. I'm guessing you already love Jesus and the subject of His coming is of great interest to you. That gives you a lot in common with all of the Apostles! James instructs us in James 5:8, "You also be patient. Establish your hearts, for the coming of the Lord is at hand." In Titus 2:13, Paul said, "Looking for the blessed hope and glorious appearing of our great God and Savior, Jesus Christ..." He frequently used the word "appearing" as a reference to the Second Coming in his epistles. In Colossians 3:4, he states, "When Christ who is our life appears, then you also will appear with Him in glory." Paul charges Timothy, in First Timothy 6:14, "that you keep this commandment without spot, blameless until our Lord Jesus Christ's appearing…" In First Thessalonians 2:19, Paul declares, "For what is our hope, or joy, or crown of rejoicing? Is it not even you in the presence of our Lord Jesus Christ at His coming?" Peter, in First Peter 5:4, expressed the blessed hope this way: "…and when the Chief Shepherd appears, you will receive the crown of glory that does not fade away." We find the apostle John expressing the same anticipation of Christ's appearing in First John 2:28. He says, "And now, little children, abide in Him, that when He appears, we may have confidence and not be ashamed before Him at His coming."

Every Holy Communion service that you have attended has mentioned the future coming of the Lord Jesus. First Corinthians 11:26 says, "For as often as you eat this bread and drink this cup, you proclaim the Lord's death till He comes." Note: *till He comes*! Scripture is filled with reminders that He will come again. First Thessalonians 3:13 says, "…so that He may establish your hearts blameless in holiness before our God and Father at the coming of our Lord Jesus Christ with all His saints. Second Thessalonians 1:10 describes that day for us, "…when He comes, in that Day, to be glorified in His saints and to be admired among all those who believe, because our testimony among you was believed." The writer of Hebrews adds, in Hebrews 9:28, "…To those who eagerly wait for Him He will appear a second time, apart from sin, for salvation." You, like the Apostles, are one of those who "eagerly wait for Him" to appear a "second time." You love to read and talk about His appearing; and so do I. I especially like to talk about the Rapture.

The Rapture

"So, Doc, you're one of those who believe in a Rapture." That's the conversation starter I usually get from liberal theologians. Invariably, the emphasis in their remark is on the word *those*. And quite frequently, the next statement is, "You know, of course, that the word is not in the Bible." (I'm thinking, "That depends upon whether or not you can read a Latin Bible," but I don't go there.) My answer (with a smile) normally is, "So, *you* are one of those who believe in the Trinity. You know, of course, that the word is not in the Bible." And then a good back-and-forth exchange follows. I find doctrinal dialogue among scholars stimulating. Almost always, I learn something. Yet, my greatest, single most reliable source of information is the Bible itself. Let me assure you, the event we call the Rapture is well-established in biblical prophecy. First, however, we should explain how the Rapture fits into Second Coming prophecy.

The Bible contains hundreds of prophecies of events recorded long before they occurred. There have been, and continue to be, amazingly precise fulfillments, recorded throughout history. The Bible holds an abundance of information about the end of this age. In fact, at least 1,845 verses refer to a Second Coming of Christ. That amounts to one out of every thirty verses in the entire Bible. In these passages, there are two differently described scenarios of the Second Coming. These apply to two different phases of the general event of the Second Coming. According to the Bible, in the end-time there will be a Rapture of the Church and a short but intense time of Great Tribulation on Earth; to be followed by the glorious return, which is properly called the Second Coming of Christ. Since some readers may not be aware of the distinctions made in Scripture concerning the two aspects of the Second coming, we will briefly introduce some key scriptures which will be discussed more fully later in this book.

In premillennial theology, the Rapture of the Church is the first phase of the Second Coming. The most popular passages which describe it are found in John 14:1-3, First Thessalonians 4 and First Corinthians 15. This sudden and instant aspect of His coming is also alluded to in Matthew 24:43, Second Thessalonians 5:2 and Second Peter 3:10. In these passages, Jesus comes suddenly and secretly like a thief. He appears in the air, and believers (both dead and alive) are caught up to join him in the air. In one sudden moment like the twinkling of an eye, they are transformed and taken away to Heaven. The Glorious Return is the second phase of His Coming. The main passages which describe this phase are Revelation 1:7, Matthew 25:31-34, Zechariah 14:3-4 and Revelation 19:11-16. In these passages, Jesus comes in all

His majesty as our King and every eye will see Him. This part of His coming is not done in the twinkling of an eye. Instead, He comes to Earth to begin the Millennial Reign from Jerusalem. He will end the Battle of Armageddon and stand again on the Mount of Olives from which He departed. In this aspect of His coming, the saints return from Heaven with Him. Between these two "comings" there will be the awful period of the Tribulation, described in Chapters 6-18 of the Book of Revelation.

The idea of the Rapture begins early in the Bible. Enoch's translation before the Flood in Genesis 5:24 and Elijah being caught up to Heaven in Second Kings 2:11 are examples of individual "raptures." In both cases they disappeared from earth and were transported bodily into God's presence. The prophet Isaiah describes the Rapture in Isaiah 26:19-20. In the New Testament, Jesus speaks of coming for us to take us to Heaven in John 14:1-3. More of the teaching of Jesus on the subject can be found in Matthew 25:1-13, where He gives the Parable of the Ten Virgins. In Mark 13:32-37, Jesus again emphasized the suddenness of His coming. The Rapture is also taught in the epistles of Paul, mainly in the two passages previously mentioned – First Thessalonians 4 and First Corinthians 15. Paul could not say whether his experience was a bodily transport or not, but in Second Corinthians 12 he related an account of being caught up to Heaven. In Revelation, John describes the church age, then tells us of things which will be "hereafter," and concludes with the glorious return of Jesus and the saints. In the main body of Revelation, the church seems to be absent from earth. From Genesis to Revelation, God's Word invites us to joyfully anticipate the Rapture.

Signs

Before the Rapture, there will be a stunning season of fulfillment of many Bible prophecies. These prophecies, I believe, are intended by the Lord to be signs (signals) to us that we are now in that season; or soon will be. Because many of the signs are tied to promises of new bodies, a new earth, new heavens and a New Jerusalem, we will also discuss these exciting aspects near the end of this book. My hope for you is that, as we explore these added dimensions of the prophetic passages together, you will find your focus shifting upward. Whatever present pains that exist in your life will become easier to endure or to overcome, because you know they won't last – but you will. The meaning of current events will no longer be as perplexing. In your heart will be a settled answer to the frequently asked question: "What on Earth is happening?"

We begin this study with an examination of exactly what Jesus said in His apocalyptic discourse on the Mount of Olives when asked what were to be the signs of His coming, and of the end of the age. We will see a group of signs that He gave to help us watch and be ready for the Rapture. Then we will also identify another group of signs mentioned in the same discourse which are to precede the time of the end, or His glorious Return. Then we will turn our attention to a large body of prophecy connected by its context to the time of the "last days." There are many signs associated simply with the last days. Near the end of this book, we will deal with several parables which Jesus gave concerning the Second Coming, and with prayers which believers should pray as they anticipate that blessed event.

My personal study on the subject of the Second Coming has led me to closely examine the time of the "last days" described by the Old

Testament prophets. The same expression was used by Jesus, Paul, Peter and John. I have concluded that in these days, we have crossed a prophetic threshold that puts us within the general time period of the "last days." This means to me that, more than ever, each of us must embrace our destiny and live out our assigned roles in this prophetic era. We need more than ever to focus on the purpose for which we were born and for which we are kept alive. We should abandon worldly ambitions that leave us empty and find true satisfaction in the destinies which God designed for us – destinies to be lived out in the power of the Holy Spirit.

A Neglected Topic

Amazingly, in this time when there is a high probability of the Second Coming, the subject receives low emphasis in pulpits of modern churches. Jesus may be ready, but much of His church is not! Certainly, the world in general has never really expected Jesus Christ to return. But post-modernity churches in Western culture have also set aside the notion of the personal return of Jesus Christ in favor of popular theologies such as Liberation Theology, Prosperity Theology, The Power of Positive Thinking, and "Kingdom Now" Theology. Half a century ago, there was a great deal of attention in churches on the Second Coming, both in preaching and in worship. Now it is too often the case that churches have exchanged a focus on the eternal for a focus on the temporal. What happened?

The Latin term, *ignoti nulla cupido*, sums up the answer. It means "we don't want what we can't see." It comes from *Ars Amatoria*, where Ovid's thought means literally "no desire (exists) for a thing unknown."[7] Neglect in the seminaries leads to neglect in the pulpit.

Two generations of pastors have been trained for ministry without much exposure to sound teaching on Second Coming theology. Though a major topic in the Bible, it is unwisely considered in some quarters to be too controversial and too divisive. The resulting silence has been heard in the pew, and congregations turn their minds to other things. But how could simple pulpit neglect bring such a complete change in the pew?

Part of the answer lies in a changed hymnology. Over time, a church becomes what it sings. Its theology is shaped by what it does or does not sing. Today old hymns that were rich in the theology of Heaven itself have been largely discarded. They are now all but completely replaced by repetitive choruses, which in large degree are more theologically shallow. Almost unknown now are the once-popular hymns, "When the Roll is Called Up Yonder," "When We All Get to Heaven," "When the Morning Comes," and "I'll Fly Away." For more than two centuries, great compositions given to the church through the inspiration of the Holy Spirit stirred the very souls of worshipers to think of Heaven and the return of the King of Kings.

George Frederic Handel in 1741 went without food for 24 days as he passionately worked with a quill pen writing the musical notes and harmonies of the majestic "Messiah." After completing the closing lines of the Hallelujah Chorus, he confided with tear-stained face to friends that, while writing, he felt as though he could see all of Heaven before him.[8] Worship choruses sung today sometimes mention Heaven; but seldom come to us through writers who are as deeply consumed with thoughts of Heaven as was Handel. Music has a way of moving theology from the head into the heart. The Church knows that Jesus promised to return and to take us to Heaven. But without the reinforcement of a consistent hymnology, and without much teaching about Heaven, the minds of modern Christians are left to drift to lesser themes. Our hearts do not feel what our heads know about Heaven. Still, I believe that the signs of His coming include world-shaking events which will awaken sleeping saints. I am persuaded that there will yet be a great worldwide revival of the Church, and that it will involve a return to a hymnology which embraces the subjects of Heaven and the glorious return of Jesus Christ.

As end-time events on the world scene rapidly unfold before us now, our own spirits should tell us that this is the season of His coming – and that it is our season! It's our time to shine. The light of our testimony should shine more brightly in the darkness of the present world. As John is told in the Book of Revelation, "The testimony of Jesus is the spirit of prophecy."[9] Any study of these prophecies should result in a greater witness to Jesus, who now gives us the peace that passes all understanding. In the power of His Spirit we should live more purposefully, work more faithfully, and pray more fervently. Jesus *is* Lord, and He *is coming!*

Above all, we need to get a grasp of who Jesus is. In the early eighties, I wrote a weekly series of articles called "Rapture Notes" for a church newsletter. In the article for January 15, 1980, I listed all the names and titles that I could find ascribed to Jesus in Scripture. The title of the article was, "Guess Who's Coming!" Here is the list.

> Alpha and Omega, Author and Finisher, Anointed, the Amen, Ancient of Days, Advocate, the One Altogether Lovely, All in All, Almighty, Beginning and the End, Bishop of Our Souls, the Branch of Righteousness, Bright and Morning Star, Bread of

God, Bread of Life, Living Bread, the Bridegroom, Balm of Gilead, Beloved Son of God, Christ, Chief Cornerstone, Counselor, Chosen, Consolation of Israel, the Captain of Our Salvation, Carpenter of Nazareth, Chief Among Ten Thousand, Christ, Crown of Glory, Creator of All Things, the Chief Shepherd, Day Star, Day Spring, Our Daysman, Desire of All Nations, Door, Deliverer, Everlasting Father, Emmanuel, Express Image, Ensign of the People, Excellent, First Begotten, First and the Last, Foundation, Friend, Faithful and True, Fountain of Forgiveness, Friend of Sinners, Firstfruits of the Resurrection, the Faithful Witness, Firstborn of Every Creature, Fairest among Ten Thousand, Governor, Great God, Good Shepherd, Gift of God, Glory of Israel, Good Master, Great Light, Great Prophet, Head, Head of the Corner, Headstone, Holy One, Hiding Place, Horn of Salvation, Heir, Hope of Glory, Hidden Manna, Helper, Highest, Hope of Israel, Head of the Body, Heir of All Things, Head of the Church, High Tower, I Am, Intercessor, Immortal, Invisible, Image of the Invisible God, Jesus, Jesus of Nazareth, Just One, Judge, King, King Eternal, King of Glory, King of Israel, King of Kings, King over all the Earth, Keeper, King of Saints, Lord, Lord and Master, Lord and Savior, Lord of Hosts, Lord God, Lord Jesus Christ, Lord of Glory, Lord of Peace, A Light, Lamb, Lamb of God, Lily of the Valleys, Life, Last Adam, Lord from Heaven, Lord of Lords, Lawgiver, Lamb in the Midst of the Throne,

Lion of Judah, Lord Over All, True Light, Light of Men, Lord of the Sabbath, Light of the Gentiles, Light of Israel, Leader, Mediator, Most Holy, Morning Star, Might God, Minister of the Sanctuary, Minister of the Circumcision, Minister of the Covenant, Messiah, Man of Sorrows, Messenger of the Covenant, Nazarene, Only Begotten Son of God, Ointment Poured Forth, Overcomer, Our Peace, An Offering, Our Hope, Our Savior, Offspring of David, Our Passover, Our Great High Priest, Prophet of the Highest, Prince of Life, Prince of Peace, Power of God, Purifier, Propitiation, the Great Physician, Potentate, Quickening Spirit, Root of David, Rock, Redeemer, Ransom, Rose of Sharon, Refiner, Righteousness, Righteous Judge, Righteous Branch, Redemption, Resurrection and the Life, Refuge from the Storm, Restorer, Seed of the Woman, Seed of Abraham, Seed of David, Son of the Highest, Son of God, A Tried Stone, Precious Cornerstone, Stumbling Stone, Stone Which Builders Rejected, Stone Cut Out of the Mountain Without Hands, Living Stone, Salvation, Son of Man, Savior, Son of Righteousness, Second Adam, Sower, Sanctification, Scepter, Shiloh, Servant of Jehovah, Sun of Righteousness, Stronghold, Sure Foundation, Teacher, Testator, Truth, Strong Tower, Testifier, Unspeakable Gift, the True Vine, the Word, Wonderful, the Way, Well Beloved, True Witness, Wisdom, Word of God. Our Lord and Saviour Jesus Christ! That's who is coming!

END NOTES FOR CHAPTER ONE

1. Lee Smolin, *The Trouble With Physics*. (NY: Houghton Mifflin Company, 2006), 241
2. Revelation 10:5-7, NIV
3. James Russell Lowell, in *Bartlett's Familiar Quotations*, 15th ed. (Boston: Little, Brown and Co., 1980), 567
4. Ecclesiastes 3:11, NIV
5. Jamie Buckingham in *The Rapture Book* by Doug Chatham. (Monroeville, PA: Whitaker House, 1974), 7
6. Second Peter 3:3b, 4a NIV
7. Eugene Ehrlich, *Amo, Amas, Amat and More*. (NY: Harper & Row, 1985), 149
8. Walter Walker, *Extraordinary Encounters With God.* (Ann Arbor: Servant Publications, 1997), 70
9. Revelation 19:10b KJV

Chapter Two

THE SECOND COMING IS A BIBLICAL EVENT

Loving the Truth Prevents Deception

CHECK OUT YOUR worldview. Does it *really* line up with the Bible? A worldview is a good thing to have. It shapes who you are and how you perceive life. Without a worldview, you'd be a vegetable! But having a worldview not based on truth leads to disappointment and even dysfunctionality. "Truth," as many of my students will recall, can be defined as "knowledge which never has to be adjusted." The Holy Bible is a book of truth, and it presents a certain worldview. In the Bible-based worldview, the Second Coming of Jesus Christ is a very real event, always on the horizon. How does your personal, practical, day-by-day worldview line up with God's Word? Keep that question in mind as you read this chapter.

The entire Bible anticipates the Day of the Lord, which begins with the Second Coming. The world's earliest prophecy about the Second Coming was uttered by Enoch, the seventh man from Adam in the line of Seth. He said, "See, the Lord is coming with thousands upon thousands of his holy ones."[1] Daniel, Zechariah and other prophets described His second coming. Jesus said He was coming back. His apostles wrote that He was coming again. Angels said as He ascended that He was coming back. The last three sayings of Jesus in Revelation are "I come quickly." We are taught in the Lord's Prayer to pray that God's kingdom will come; that His will be done on Earth as it is in Heaven. Paul prayed, "Maranatha!" (Our Lord, Come!). The last prayer of the Bible is "Even so, Come."

As the prophet Hosea put it, "My people are destroyed from lack of knowledge."[2] Neglect of teaching on the Second Coming has led many to falsely assume that a bodily return of the Lord Jesus is not necessarily biblical. Some say that the actual words, "The Second Coming," are not in the English Bible. Of course, neither are the words "Trinity" or "Rapture" or "Immaculate Conception." But all are major biblical concepts. All are vital to other doctrines. An understanding of the Second Coming is essential to effective Christian living. But, first things first!

We will begin by pointing to several key prophetic passages which establish the Second Coming as a biblical doctrine. These passages are some of the "truth" which is mentioned in the following prophecy about the Antichrist, found in the second chapter of Second Thessalonians.

> The coming of the lawless one will be in accordance with the work of Satan displayed in all kinds of counterfeit miracles, signs and wonders, and in every sort of evil that deceives those who are perishing. They will perish because they refused to love the

> truth and be saved. For this reason God sends them a powerful delusion so that they will believe the lie and so that all will be condemned who have not believed the truth but have delighted in wickedness.[3]

There is a satanic plot to keep your mind off the Second Coming. The devil is lying and deceiving, with the special intent of causing those who are perishing to reject the truth by which they could be saved. But the scriptures are clear: Jesus said, "I will come again."[4] He said repeatedly in the gospels, "Watch and be ready!" It is wise for us to know and love the truth. Armed with the truth, we cannot be deceived. Believers in Jesus know only one source of truth: the Word of God. It tells us what will really happen in the last days. Therefore, let us revisit some of major prophesies which point to the Second Coming and which establish us in the truth – the truth which we must either wholeheartedly embrace or risk deception by the enemy. These four key prophesies have been selected because they describe the Second Coming in essentially the same words. This series of prophecy sources given here are foundational to all that we will discuss in this book. They are:

- Prophesied by Daniel
- Prophesied by Jesus
- Prophesied by Paul
- Prophesied by John

Prophesied by Daniel

A key prophecy of the Second Coming was by the Hebrew prophet Daniel who lived and prophesied in the first half of the sixth century

B.C. He is considered one of the greatest of the Hebrew prophets. He describes a series of future kingdoms, ending with one which encompasses all nations and is ruled by a king whose dominion is forever. Here is part of the prophecy found in the seventh chapter of Daniel.

> I saw in the night visions, and behold, one like the Son of man came with the clouds of heaven, and came to the Ancient of days, and they brought him near before him. And there was given him dominion, and glory, and a kingdom, that all people, nations, and languages, should serve him: his dominion is an everlasting dominion, which shall not pass away, and his kingdom that which shall not be destroyed.[5]

This is the first biblical mention of a special term which applies to Jesus Christ: "Son of man." It is set in the context of Daniel's larger prophetic vision of four beasts which represented four world empires which would stretch from his time to the time of the eternal kingdom described here in verse 14. The Empires were Babylon, Persia, Greece and Rome, with a remnant of the latter empire eventually developing into a confederacy of ten kingdoms. The one who rises to power as ruler of all these kingdoms will oppose God and eventually be destroyed by the eternal kingdom of the Son of man. (See verses 19-27 of Daniel 7).

This prophecy of Daniel is the central prophecy which Jesus uses in His earthly ministry to point to Himself as the Son of Man, the favorite title He used of Himself. This title as used by Jesus is found 78 times in the Gospels, as well as in Acts 7:56, Revelation 1:13 and 14:14. In every instance, Jesus is designated by Himself or by others as the

God-Man. Daniel's prophetic vision shows the Son of Man coming with the clouds of heaven and being given an everlasting dominion over all people, nations and languages. The repeated reiteration of this event by Jesus and the New Testament writers strongly reinforce the idea of a literal, rather than symbolic, fulfillment.

Let's analyze this. First, Daniel saw One "like a son of man." In other words, the One he saw was like a human in appearance, in contrast to the four beasts just seen in this vision. Second, he saw Him "coming with the clouds". In apocalyptic language, this was symbolic of a divine warrior – not a mere human. He was brought before the "Ancient of Days," referring to the Deity whose appearance upon a fiery throne has just been described. This means that His personhood is distinct from the Ancient of Days (God the Father). He is given authority, glory and sovereign power. After His resurrection, Jesus said, "All power is given unto me in heaven and in earth."[6]

To continue the analysis: in Daniel's vision, all people, nations and languages worship Jesus. This is not yet, but when His kingdom comes. His dominion is everlasting. This means that He lives forever, or else His dominion could not. Unlike the preceding kingdoms of Babylon, Persia, Greece and Rome, this kingdom is forever. Your eternal life is based upon the "eternalness" of Christ and His kingdom. Once you have been translated out of the kingdom of Satan, you live forever in the assurance that your new kingdom is yours to enjoy forever.

Prophesied by Jesus

The greatest of all the prophets is Jesus, Himself. Jesus prophesied during His trial before the High Priest that He would come again. Only hours before Jesus was hung on the Cross, he made a statement about Himself to the head of the Jewish religion. In that statement, recorded in three Gospels, Jesus clearly identified Himself as the Son of Man mentioned in Daniel's prophecy. Dragged by the temple police to the palace of Caiaphas, Jesus faced false accusations before a hastily assembled session of the Sanhedrin. The High Priest asked Him directly if He was the Christ. His response convinced these Jewish scholars that he was using Daniel's prophecy to identify Himself as the Son of God. ...Again the high priest questioned Him, "Are You the Messiah, the Son of the Blessed One?" "I am," said Jesus, "and all of you will see the Son of Man seated at the right hand of the Power and coming with the clouds of heaven."[7]

Jesus precedes His reference to Daniel 7:13-14 with a reference to a prophecy given in Psalms 110:1. "The Lord says to my Lord: 'Sit at my right hand until I make your enemies a footstool for your feet.'"(NIV) Therefore, in one statement, Jesus distinguishes two of His future actions as Son of Man. The first is that He will resume His seat in Heaven, and the second is that He is coming again to Earth to reign. Since the chief priests had already decided not to acknowledge Jesus as the Messiah, they now declared this utterance by Jesus to be blasphemy.

On the Mount of Olives just the day before his arrest, some disciples asked Jesus what would be the signs of His coming and of the end of the age. The composite record of His responses can be seen in the different but complementary accounts mainly found in three chapters in the Gospels. We will later examine those chapters (Mark 13, Matthew 23 and Luke 21) to see a list of signs of His coming. Jesus on that occasion said His coming would be like a flash of lightning. He identified that coming with a prophecy in Zechariah, which contains the words, "they shall look upon me whom they have pierced."[8]

Jesus continued in the same discourse to the disciples, "And then shall appear the sign of the Son of man in heaven: and then shall all the tribes of the earth mourn, and they shall see the Son of man coming in the clouds of heaven with power and great glory." [9] This last phrase was another reference to the same prophecy in Daniel 7:13, which we have just examined. Clearly, Jesus was intentionally identifying Himself as the Son of Man in Daniel 7, a Person believed by the Jews to be the Son of God.

Two important conclusions should be made here. First, Jesus said He is the Son of Man who is coming in the clouds of heaven. That means that He is the One who will have an everlasting dominion over all people, nations and languages. Second, Jesus said that He will come again in great power and glory. That means He will come in sovereign majesty and with spectacular splendor. The lowly Jesus of Nazareth will return as King of all Kings and Lord of all Lords and reign forever. He is coming again! That is a prophecy made by the greatest prophet of all time, Jesus Christ.

Here is another brief analysis. Jesus presents Himself as the Son of Man. This is not a reference to His human nature, but to a title which refers to the promised Messiah. He will sit at the right hand of the Power (NIV: "Mighty One"). In other words, He will be seated at the right hand of God. As Stephen, the first Christian martyr, was being stoned to death, he saw Jesus *standing* on the right hand of God.[10] (This might indicate that, though He had been seated, He rose to welcome Stephen). Further analysis of this passage shows that He will come with (on, in) the clouds of heaven. The idea that He comes with the clouds is a symbolic reference to the conquest of a mighty king riding a chariot ahead of a great army, stirring up clouds of dust. His coming will be also a conquest which will forever end the tyranny of the Antichrist.

Before we leave this prophecy of Jesus, note the sequence that He gives to end-time events. Jesus said, "Immediately after the tribulation of those days; the sun shall be darkened, and the moon will not shed its light; and the stars will fall from the sky, and the celestial powers shall be shaken."[11] Then He says we will see Him coming in the clouds. Because this is all part of one statement, we can see that the return to which Jesus refers will take place immediately *after* the Tribulation period. This does not seem to be a description of a Rapture which *precedes* the Tribulation, but of a glorious Return which follows the Tribulation. The collapse of the visible cosmos will accompany this particular appearing of Jesus in the sky; therefore it should not be confused with His appearing in the sky to receive the saints in the Rapture.

Prophesied by Paul

The great apostle Paul gave us another key prophecy concerning the Second Coming. The apostle penned his epistles to the Thessalonian Christians during a time of great persecution and anxiety. They anticipated the coming of the Lord at any time. Yet, during those perilous times some believers had already died. They were concerned that the ones who had died would miss the coming of the Lord. In First Thessalonians 4, Paul assures them that those who died will be coming back with Jesus when He returns. Their dead bodies will rise first to meet them and the Lord in the air.[12] Paul goes on to give this powerful prophecy: "For the Lord Himself shall descend from heaven with a shout, with the archangel's voice, and with the trumpet of God, and the dead in Christ will rise first. Then we who are still alive will be caught up together with them in the clouds to meet the Lord in the air; and so we will always be with the Lord."[13]

We should note here that Paul is clearly describing a different phase of the Lord's coming than the prophecy of Jesus which we have just examined. This speaks of a time when the Lord only returns for the saints, and when they will leave the earth to meet Him in the air. It describes twin events: a resurrection and a rapture. Paul has more to say about this coming of the Lord in an epistle to the Corinthians: "Listen, I tell you a mystery: we will not all sleep, but we will all be changed – in a flash, in the twinkling of an eye, at the last trumpet. For the trumpet will sound, the dead will be raised imperishable, and we will be changed."[14]

The coming of Jesus described here will be instantaneous and without warning. It comes without the preliminary events of the Tribulation and collapse of the solar system. This prophecy refers in particular to the first phase of the Lord's return, described by scholars as the Rapture of the Church. We are required to be faithfully alert and prepared for Him to come at any time. In Mark's gospel, the record shows that on the same occasion in which He described His glorious return, Jesus also described this sudden phase of His coming.

> No one knows about that day or hour, not even the angels in heaven, nor the Son, but only the Father. Be on guard! Be alert! You do not know when that time will come. It's like a man going away: He leaves his house and puts his servants in charge, each with

> his assigned task, and tells the one at the door to keep watch. Therefore keep watch because you do not know when the owner of the house will come back – whether in the evening, or at midnight, or when the rooster crows, or at dawn. If he comes suddenly, do not let him find you sleeping. What I say to you, I say to everyone: "Watch."[15]

Paul's prophesies repeatedly mention the sounding of the trumpet of God. In First Corinthians 15, he specifically calls it the "last" trumpet. Armies in biblical times moved according to trumpet signals. There was a series of trumpet blasts prior to each march or prior to a charge into battle. There would be various signals to assemble to prepare armor and take up weapons, to mount horses, or to fall into formation. The *last* trumpet, however, was always a signal to move out! In the context of Paul's prophecy, the Lord's coming will be accompanied by a trumpet's tremendous blast, heard by all believers. One might insist that everyone, including unbelievers, would hear such a loud sound. How then could it be a secret coming, as some describe the Rapture? In response, we can point to instances in the Bible where heavenly sounds were heard clearly by some and not by others. In John 12:29, God had just spoken from heaven, but some of the crowd thought only that it had thundered. It is unlikely that those who are unsaved will be spiritually equipped or attuned to hear this awesome call.

Prophesied by John

We turn now to a prophecy in the Book of Revelation, written by the apostle John. John the beloved disciple is a unique character among all the apostles of the New Testament. He was one of the inner circle of three disciples closest to Jesus. He became the caregiver for Mary the mother of Jesus. He was the last surviving member of original 12 disciples and served as Bishop at Ephesus, overseeing the seven churches of Asia. God chose to entrust and inspire John with the closing scriptures of the canon of the New Testament. Therefore, John's writings are of tremendous significance to us.

The Book of Revelation is a series of apocalyptic visions given to the aged apostle John around A.D. 96, while he was exiled on the island of Patmos. Written during a time of intense persecution and martyrdom of Christians throughout the Roman Empire, it is full of promises to believers, and centers around the Second Coming. In many ways, it is a fitting conclusion to the New Testament and to the entire Bible, for it describes the end of the age and the future eternal state. The theme of the book is announced in verse 7 of the first chapter. "Look, he is coming with the clouds, and every eye will see him, even those who pierced him; and all the peoples of the earth will mourn because of him. So shall it be! Amen."[16] Here, John is simply referring to the exact words in previous prophesies by Zechariah and Jesus.

Once more, in the final book of the Bible, the Holy Spirit is reminding us of this central prophetic theme: "He is coming with the clouds!" John's emphasis in Revelation is upon the glorious return of Jesus. He will be seen by all people, yet one specific group is singled out: "...those who pierced him..." We will return later in this book to the eschatological role of the Jewish people and their conversion to Christ as the Hebrew Messiah. For the present, we note that John goes on to say that *all* peoples of the earth will mourn. This will come at the end of the final rebellion on the earth, when all people groups which are on the planet at that time will be held accountable for their sins.

The climax of the book of Revelation comes in Chapter 11, verse 15. The seventh angel sounded his trumpet, and there were loud voices in heaven, which said: "The kingdom of the world has become the kingdom of our Lord and of His Christ, and He will reign for ever and ever."[17] This is when Daniel's prophecy is finally fulfilled. This is when the last of all kingdoms will be established, the one which will endure forever. The last phrase here in verse 15 is the source for the words in the wonderful Hallelujah Chorus of Handel's "Messiah." He shall reign for ever and ever!

The Coming King is Our King Now

As a believer in Christ, the King of the coming kingdom is One whom you already know and love. He is the One in whom you have forgiveness of sins and eternal life. He is the One who has already made you a citizen of His kingdom. You should be giving thanks, as Paul prayed for the Colossian believers,

> ...giving thanks to the Father, who has qualified you to share in the inheritance of the saints in the kingdom of light. For he has rescued us from the dominion of darkness and brought us into the kingdom of the Son he loves, in whom we have redemption, the forgiveness of sins.[18]

Vance Havner put it this way: "We are not just looking for something to happen; we are looking for Someone to come! And when these things begin to come to pass, we are not to drop our heads in discouragement or shake our heads in despair, but rather lift up our heads in delight."[19] A sincere conviction that Christ is coming will result in an upward attitude.

Our more casual conversations reveal our real interests. Normally, when among friends, we speak most frequently of whatever is a major excitement in our hearts. We had an old saying in the community where I grew up – a community of homes without electricity and dependent upon water drawn by hand from wells. We said, "What's down in the well will come up in the bucket." We meant that whatever you were thinking about would come out in your speech. Which leads to me to the following question: Are you so excited about the Lord's coming that you speak of it frequently? This goes back to your personal worldview, which we mentioned as we began this chapter. What does your casual speech say about your worldview?

Jesus our King is "King of Kings" even now, exalted far above every earthly ruler. He sits at the right hand of God, where He is now "… far above all rule and authority, power and dominion, and every title that can be given, not only in this present age but also in the one to come."[20] When he returns, you won't have to learn any new laws or rules to try to fit into His kingdom! The same Kingdom rules by which you now live will still apply: love God with all your heart and love your neighbor as yourself! Won't it be wonderful when everyone really does that?

You should say often to yourself, "I already have a King. I'm already in His Kingdom." When He comes, that won't change. But everything else will! Your health, your hardships, your heartaches – all will be changed. In these turbulent times we should discipline ourselves to get our mind off things which are temporary, and set our thoughts on things which are eternal. In any trial or trouble you can say, "This won't last, but I will!" If we just devote ourselves to "seek first the kingdom of God," everything else eventually falls into place. A verse in Romans 8, previously mentioned, states the basic Kingdom principle which applies here. If you love God and live according to His purposes, all things will work together for good (Romans 8:28).

In this chapter we have reviewed four principal prophesies by Daniel, Jesus, Paul and John; all of which are predictions of Jesus coming in the clouds. These alone are sufficient to establish the Second Coming as a thoroughly biblical event. They were selected because they demonstrate a unity of Scripture and trace a consistent prediction. The Son of Man is coming with the clouds in great power and glory. While there are dozens of other prophecies which will be considered later in this book, this review has been presented so that we can build upon the foundational premise that the Second Coming is thoroughly biblical. It will happen. Therefore, we should anticipate it literally as history's greatest event. With this foundational understanding, we are ready to move on in the next chapter and identify a rather large group of signs, which the Bible says will signal the time of the Second Coming.

ENDNOTES FOR CHAPTER TWO

1. Jude 14
2. Hosea 4:6a NIV
3. Second Thessalonians 2:9-12 NIV
4. John 14:3b KJV
5. Daniel 7:13-14 KJV
6. Matthew 28:18b KJV
7. Mark 14:61b-62 CSB
8. Zechariah 12:10b KJV
9. Matthew 24:30 CSB
10. Acts 7:56
11. Matthew 24:29 CSB
12. First Thessalonians 4:13-15
13. First Thessalonians 4:16-17 CSB
14. First Corinthians 15:51-52 NIV
15. Mark 13:32-37 NIV
16. Revelation 1: 7 NIV
17. Revelation 11:15 NIV
18. Colossians 1:12-14 NIV
19. Vance Havner, *In Times Like These.* (Old Tappan, NJ: Fleming H. Revell Co., 1969), 29
20. Ephesians 1:21 NIV

Chapter Three

SIGNS PRECEDING THE END IN THE OLIVET DISCOURSE

The Olivet Discourse

NOW AS HE sat on the Mount of Olives opposite the temple, Peter, James, John, and Andrew asked Him privately,

"Tell us, when will these things be? And what will be the sign when all of these things will be fulfilled?" – Mark 13:3-4

Now as He sat on the Mount of Olives, the disciples came to Him privately, saying, "Tell us, when will these things be? And what will be the sign of Your coming, and of the end of the age?" – Matthew 24:3

And when they asked Him, saying, "Teacher, but when will these things be? And what sign will there be when these things are about to take place?" – Luke 21:7

The above verses are individual snapshots of the Savior sitting on a rock on the Mount of Olives, surrounded by only four disciples. They introduce three separate Gospel accounts of the Lord's teaching on the season of His coming and on the end of the age. The specific occasion was really not a public gathering. It was a private session with four disciples on the afternoon of Abib 12 on the Jewish calendar, just two and one-half days before Jesus was crucified. This teaching is called the Olivet Discourse, because of the location. It is also called the Synoptic Apocalypse, because of its apocalyptic style and because it is recorded in all three Synoptic Gospels. The Synoptic Gospels, Matthew, Mark and Luke, are so called because they "see" together.

The four disciples - Peter, James, John and Andrew – had walked with Jesus up the winding road leading out of Jerusalem, across the Kidron Valley and up over the Mount of Olives. They apparently stopped to rest at a good vantage point and looked back upon the imposing magnificence of the temple. It had recently been rebuilt by King Herod, using massive stone blocks, and was widely believed to be one of the greatest buildings of the ancient world. The disciples were marveling at its construction, when Jesus commented that the days would come when not one stone would be left upon another. This triggered some questions, and their answers form the framework of the discourse.

None of the three gospel writers were present. Mark's abbreviated record is based upon the eyewitness account of Peter. Matthew takes part of his record from Mark, partly from another early written account (also accessed by Luke) and partly from his own conversations with the other disciples who were present. Luke's record is the most intentionally thorough of all. He says in the introduction to his gospel that he has undertaken to consult all the eyewitnesses. Thus, we have a collaborative collection of eyewitness accounts. This collection is found mainly in only three New Testament chapters: Matthew 24, Mark 13, and Luke 21. These three chapters contain a large number of signs which Jesus connected with the end of the age.

The questions which Jesus addressed were about the destruction of the temple ("these things"), the end of the age, and the coming of Jesus. Although each writer has the questions worded a bit differently, in all three accounts the disciples refer to "these things," using the plural. So, they were asking about the destruction of the temple and any events connected with that. During that week, they had seen Jesus purge the temple and denounce the religious establishment. They obviously connected the destruction of the temple with the end of the present time and the beginning of the new Messianic order. In the context of what Jesus had said and done the last few days, they may have thought "these things" would all transpire in the near future. To the contrary, the purpose of the discourse seems to be to show that many events – and much time – will intervene between the temple's destruction and His return.

Warning: what follows is my personal opinion. The signs are events that will demonstrate that the season of His coming is near, and that the divine plan is unfolding according to schedule. Although no timetable can be dogmatically assumed from this Discourse, there does appear to be a recognizable sequence. We can see this more easily as we separate these signs into two lists. The initial list is a series of things which will happen before "the end." The last group is of things that actually happen when "the end shall come." The sign which culminates the first list is that of the Gospel being preached in all the world as a witness to all nations. The sign which begins the last list is the Abomination of Desolation which appears in the temple.

The first group of signs can be assigned the period which precedes the time of the end, called by Jesus "the beginning of sorrows" (KJV) or "birth pains" (NIV).[1] This metaphor of the first pains of childbirth indicates signals that something is about to happen soon. The second group, in the view of most conservative scholars, belongs to the time of the end that is called the Tribulation Period and which is described in much of the book of Revelation.

You can likely get several contradictory opinions about how the signs can be grouped, and how we should interpret each of these signs. There is plenty of room for differing interpretations. But we dare not lose sight of the significance of the signs in the Olivet Discourse. Please remember that the most important thing is that they are signs. And they are signs of either the end of the age, or of the return of Jesus, or both. It is less important to agree upon whether or not the signs can be grouped into those before and after the sign of the Gospel going into all the world. As we said earlier, this is book is not about timetables, but about times. The signs, when compared to current developments, are difficult to dismiss. History is heading somewhere – fast!

There are two great unknowns in the Discourse. First, it is impossible in our human judgment to qualify and quantify exactly when we shall have preached the Gospel to the whole world – therefore it could happen at any time. However, it seems clear to me that Jesus had some specific in mind; and that when it happens, the end will come. Second, we cannot know precisely what is meant by the "end" which Jesus has in view. Does He mean the start of a series of end-time events which belong to the Tribulation Period, or does He mean His glorious return at the end of the entire Tribulation Period? If the pre-tribulation theologians are right, Jesus is referring to the

Rapture which triggers the Tribulation period. If not, then there are two other views which may be correct. One has to do with a mid-tribulation Rapture, while the other view combines the Rapture with the glorious return and makes the Second Coming a single event. In all of these views, however, the end is imminent when the Gospel has been preached to the entire world.

The Eight Signs in the Beginning of Sorrows Period

The first list of signs starts in Matthew 24, where Jesus indicates some signs that are likened to a time of early birth pains. Verses 5-8 contain five of them: false messiahs, wars and preparations for war, ethnic conflicts, famines, and earthquakes. Jesus goes on to say in the next verse that all these are the beginning of birth pains (the KJV uses "sorrows"). All of these were easily fulfilled in the next 50 or 100 years, but apparently would also continue to occur throughout the period. As the list resumes, we begin to see other signs that were soon fulfilled, but that also seem to have eschatological overtones – other fulfillments on a greater scale near the time of the end.

The next thing Jesus mentions is the persecution and martyrdom which these disciples would face. However, He added some words which placed this sign in the distant future. He says they will be hated by *all nations* because of Him, which seems to indicate a more universal hatred of all disciples of Jesus. This becomes more plausible when connected to verse 10 of Matthew 24, which begins with the words, "At that time," indicating a specific time, and also linking the persecution in verse 9 with the other two signs in verses 10-14. The next sign is loss of love. In that time, many will turn from faith in Christ. Their love for Him and for one another will grow cold.

Because of the activity of false prophets they will hate and betray one another. The final sign belonging to the Beginning of Sorrows, the time which immediately precedes the time of the end, is the sign of the Gospel being preached in all the world as a witness to all ethnic groups.

Now, let's put them together.

- False Messiahs
- Wars and Preparations for War
- Ethnic Conflicts
- Famines
- Earthquakes
- Persecution
- Loss of Love for Christ
- The Gospel Preached in all the World

In the Matthew account, it is precisely in the statement of the eighth sign that Jesus says, "and then the end will come." Mark puts the preaching of the Gospel to all nations in the context of his description of the universal persecution of disciples. Luke inserts that during the persecution, disciples will have the opportunity to witness before kings and governors. In each case, the preaching of the Gospel to all nations comes at the end of the period called Beginning of Sorrows.

Have these signs now been fulfilled? Or will they yet be fulfilled in some greater way just before Jesus comes? There have been many false messiahs, and there are some now on the world scene who claim to be Christ. There have been many wars or preparations for war. There are even more today. Ethnic conflicts have existed throughout history; mass genocides such as committed against one-and-a half million Armenians by the Turks, or against six million Jews by the Nazis. In recent times, Cambodia, Croatia, Sudan, Indonesia, Kenya, India and Sudan have had their ethnic killing zones. In many parts of the world, inter-tribal ethnic hostilities rage now – at least 57 armed conflicts. Famines have always followed wars and natural disasters. There is much hunger in the world today. One out of every three children on earth will go to sleep without supper tonight.

Massive earthquakes have also been common since the time of this prophecy. They are common now. Hardly a week goes by, but in the news somewhere in the world are earthquakes. Persecution of Christians began in the Book of Acts and continues today. In fact, more Christians are dying for their faith in our lifetime than died in all the Roman persecutions. For example, in August of 2008, anti-Christian persecution exploded in Orissa State, India. Hundreds of homes were destroyed; many churches bombed and burned. Dozens of people were martyred, including innocent children. Thousands of Christians lost everything, fleeing into jungles for safety. They are now housed in relief camps or hiding with relatives. In Iraq, persecution of Christians which was widespread under Saddam Hussein, was recently renewed in a northern province. Militia would knock on a door during the night. When the man of the home opened the door, the men in uniform would ask, "Are you a Christian?" When he said, "Yes," they immediately shot him. Is the current worldwide persecution of Christians a sign of the Lord's coming?

Certainly we live in a time when many are tested, and their love for Christ is failing. It is more popular to be secular, an agnostic, a Buddhist, a Hindu, or Muslim - or anything else – than to be a Christian. All these points of view can be openly taught in U.S.

public schools, but not Christianity. Holidays belonging to other religions can be freely studied and observed in classrooms, but not Christmas. Many members of Christian churches just "blend in" with society during the workday week, rather than risk ridicule by witnessing. They remain silent rather than take unpopular stands against immorality. Throughout history, in places and times when Christians faced persecution and the threat of martyrdom, many renounced their faith. But the weakness of witness seems more widespread now than ever before. The preaching of false prophets has resulted in many today no longer having a faith for which they would be willing to die. Could it be that this is a sign of the Lord's coming?

The tension between "already" and "not yet," so common to much biblical prophecy, is especially seen here in this group of signs. This is what makes it necessary for us to watch and be ready, and to pray that we will escape all those things which will come during the Tribulation. If we could be sure that many other signs would have to be fulfilled before Jesus comes, we might be tempted to relax or even fall into apostasy. On the other hand, we do not know for sure that all these signs have not been completely fulfilled. Jesus could come at any moment now! Some scholars believe that shortly before the Second Coming, each of these signs will happen to a larger degree than every before, all at the same time. It could also be that these tragedies will simply be symptomatic of the entire age; that is, they will continue in repetitive cycles throughout history until the final sign appears.

The Eighth Sign

The eighth and final sign is made distinct in the Olivet Discourse, because Jesus said that when it happens, "then the end will come!" Most conservative scholars believe that because of its place of mention in the list of signs given by Jesus, the "end" refers to the end time which begins with the Rapture. The Rapture, according to traditional scholarship, is an initial phase of an entire group of events in the Eschaton (the group of last things). So, the end mentioned here could refer to the whole time period which includes the Rapture, Tribulation, Armageddon, Glorious Return, Millennial Reign, Great White Throne Judgment, Destruction of Earth, New Jerusalem, New Heavens and New Earth. "This gospel of the kingdom will be preached in the whole world as a testimony to all nations, and then the end will come."[2]

In my view, the end spoken of in Matthew 24:14 starts with the Rapture; and that blessed event will trigger the end time, which itself is comprised of a succession of prophesied events. These are described in the remainder of the Olivet Discourse. After this statement that the end will come, Jesus goes on to describe other signs, beginning with the Abomination of Desolation – mentioned next in Matthew. Then comes the Great Tribulation (described in much of the Book of Revelation); and following that, a cosmic collapse: the sun and moon darkened, with the stars falling. The powers of the heavens will be shaken, and then the Lord will appear in all His glory.[3] Therefore, the other signs given here are signs of the glorious Second Coming at the very end of the age. We will examine them shortly. But before leaving the period of the Beginning of Sorrows and going on to The Time of the End, we should give more attention to this pivotal eighth sign, which is the Gospel being preached to the whole world.

The number eight in the Bible is significant of new birth, new beginning, or salvation. Here, it reminds us of the great harvest of souls receiving salvation during that final worldwide witness. As we write this, the world's greatest revival may already be underway. As many as 50,000 new Christians per day are reported in China alone. More than 30,000 conversions per day are happening in parts of India. According to an article in Mission Frontiers, 100,000 new believers are "born again" each day.[4] The same article puts the number of new indigenous churches that are planted each day at 4,500. The terms "sending and receiving nations" no longer applies in today's mission work. There are now over 4,000 Third-World mission agencies,[5] many of them sending missionaries to Europe and to the United States.

In many parts of the world, the current revival of soul winning and planting churches and training disciples is going forward at a rapid rate. It is difficult to know exactly what is happening inside many of the closed nations within the "10/40 Window." That is the area of the globe extending from the Atlantic coast of Africa through the Middle East to the Pacific coast of Asia, between 10 and 40 degrees North Latitude. According to often quoted missions statistics, over 93% of the world's unreached population within this window waits for evangelization. Still, we hear persistent, widespread reports that Jesus is revealing Himself in visions in these darkened nations. Hearts are being strangely warmed in preparation for the witness of evangelistic Christians, which must come. Even now, there is a movement of the underground Chinese church to send witnesses marching westward across Asia, carrying the Gospel through the heartlands of Islam, all the way back to Jerusalem where the Gospel first began.

With the global literacy rate now at an all-time high, it is increasingly effective to distribute the Scriptures in the languages of the 10/40 Window. Large Bible publication societies with huge printing presses are dedicated to this task. Millions in these closed nations have access to short wave radio, as well as the internet. Powerful short-wave broadcasts of the Gospel in many languages are beamed daily into this area. Tens of thousands of career missionaries and their families have fanned out all over the world. In support, the combined efforts of the world's mission agencies keep an air force of over 500 planes airborne daily carrying personnel and supplies. Big hospital ships (called Mercy Ships), manned by Christian medical personnel dock at ports around the world to give aid and spread the Gospel. A flotilla of Christian hospital boats ply the Amazon, as well the island chains of the Pacific. Additionally, hundreds of thousands of church members go annually in short-term teams to support career missionaries around the globe. Like never before, we have the opportunity to see the Great Commission fulfilled in our lifetime.

Still, even with all those exciting developments, the Gospel has never yet been taken into all the world as a witness to all ethnic groups – so far as we know. For one thing, we do not all agree upon what constitutes an ethno-linguistic group, nor upon how to determine what is the minimum population of such a designation. "Ethne" is the Greek word for nations. It refers to people who are bound together by common cultural, linguistic, religious, behavioral, and biological traits. There are 2,795 such groups in the country of India alone. At the time of this writing, the Joshua Project (see joshua.project.net) lists 16,314 people groups, of which 6,739 are already reached. The numbers change almost daily. Another point of uncertainty is what we mean when we say "reached." Normally, we mean that the people group has an indigenous church capable of planting other indigenous churches, without outside help. These churches should be self-supporting, self-governing, and self-propagating.

At the current rate of effort, the whole world *could* soon be reached with the witness of the Gospel, and then the end will come! As you read this, you have a part in *how soon.* As we are told in Second Peter 3, we should be "looking for and hastening the coming of the Day of God…"[6] How does a Christian "hasten" the day of God? By being obedient! Jesus gave to all who would be His true followers, a job description – what we call The Great Commission. He said we were to go into all the world and make disciples of all nations. As a follower, you dare not disobey. Jesus said, "But why do you call me 'Lord, Lord', and do not do the things which I say?"[7] There are many ways to participate, as an evangelist, teacher, missionary, intercessor, personal witness, financial supporter, logistics support worker, translator, broadcaster, short-term team member, and a large number of other ways to serve. As Rick Warren pointed out in *The Purpose Driven Life*, we all have a purpose, and we should live our life with that as our focus. Find your purpose for being alive at this time in history, and you can soon be doing one, or several, of the things just mentioned.

An Unfinished Book

It's hard to find something new in a book. As far back as 940 B.C., the "Preacher" in Ecclesiastes was saying, "…of making many books there is no end…"[8] Like many others, I enjoy writing books. But I know that what I have written has been written before, and will be written again. "There is nothing new under the sun."[9] There is, however, one book which is unique in the universe. No man has ever read it. No duplicates exist. It's not finished yet. What is being written in it is of infinite importance to all of us. It is the Book of Life. God is writing it, and He's putting new names in it every day.

If your name is not in it, you have no access to Heaven. Jesus said that we should rejoice if our names are written in Heaven.[10] We are told that "whosoever was not found written the book of life" will be cast into the lake of fire at the Great White Throne Judgment.[11] In the message to the church at Sardis in Revelation, Jesus says, "He who overcomes shall be clothed in white garments, and I will not blot out his name from the Book of Life; but I will confess his name before my Father and before His angels."[12]

As a boy alone in the deep woods of Louisiana, I would often find old beech trees which held in their smooth bark the carved names of men who had passed that way, years before. I confess that I was fascinated by the seeming permanence of those names, and would carve my own name beside them. The carvings faded away long ago. Even the trees are gone. But there is a book in Heaven that has my name in it, and it is written with ink that never fades. A time of great trouble lies just ahead in this world. You won't survive if your name is not written in the Book of Life. But the prophet Daniel, speaking of this time of great trouble, says that those whose names are written in the book will be delivered.[13] Here's our challenge: the Book of Life is still unfinished. There are millions of names missing!

After this life, there are just two destinations. One place is Heaven, which is for those whose names are in the Lamb's Book of Life. It will be our home only if in this life we make Jesus our Lord and Savior. Heaven is the place of eternal life. The other place is the default destination: an everlasting eternity in Hell. There, the demon worms of Hell continuously devour and the flames ceaselessly torment. In the bottomless pit, there is a terrifying sensation of endlessly falling. There is eternal separation from God and all that is good. This condition continues forever with no chance of change. When Jesus comes to take us to Heaven, those who are left behind will be left out.

Jesus cares deeply, and so should we. When we walk closely enough, we will feel His heartbeat. It throbs with a passion for reaching those who do not know Him. He said, "The Son of Man has come to save that which was lost." Before He ascended, He left us in charge of making Him known. On at least three post-resurrection occasions, at three different locations, He repeated our job description. We call it the Great Commission. When we obey it, more names can be written down in Heaven. One day, the last name will be written and the great Book of Life will be finished. It will be closed, with or without our participation. But if it happens without our participation, then we have a huge problem! Remember the question of Jesus: "But why do you call Me 'Lord, Lord,' and do not do the things which I say?"[14] If you do not care about souls, and do not delight in obeying Jesus, what meaning is there in your relationship to Him? Indeed, what meaning is there to your life?

God is asking today what He asked Isaiah the prophet, "Who will go for us?" Many are hearing His call and responding in unusual circumstances. A few years ago, while I was directing the MOST (Missions Overseas Short Term) training program at Beulah Heights University, a Chinese professor attended MOST to receive this intense training in intercultural evangelism and church planting. Dr. Han (A pseudonym: we cannot use his real name.) was a new Christian, having been converted to Christ just the week before. From the People's Republic of China, he was in the U.S. for only a few weeks as an exchange instructor in one of our state universities. Prak Deetana, a member of the MOST steering committee, had led Han to a salvation experience with the Lord Jesus and then baptized him on the Sunday before the MOST training program began on Monday. After the training, Han returned to China and began to plant house churches. He now pastors over 8,000 members in dozens of secret house churches.

Life is too precious and too short to waste in wandering about. May we all find our true calling and get going, like Dr. Han. When we use Mapquest, to find an address, we sometimes have to enter the name of a known intersection of two streets. In a spiritual way, that is how you can find the will of God for your life. It will be found at the intersection of two "streets." One is "Great Commandment Street" and the other is "Great Commission Street." There, at that intersection, you will find the heartbeat of God and the meaning of your life on Earth!

ENDNOTES FOR CHAPTER THREE

1. Matthew 24:8
2. Matthew 24:14 NIV
3. Matthew 24:15-30
4. Justin Long, "Least-Reached Peoples," *Mission Frontiers* (May-June 2006), p. 8
5. Ibid.
6. Second Peter 3:12a KJV
7. Luke 6:46 KJV
8. Ecclesiastes 12:12
9. Ecclesiastes 1:9c
10. Luke 10:20
11. Revelation 20:15
12. Revelation 3:5
13. Daniel 12:1
14. Luke 6:46

Chapter Four

SIGNS DURING THE END TIME IN THE OLIVET DISCOURSE

> AND YOU WILL hear of wars and rumors of wars. See that you are not troubled; for all these things must come to pass, but the end is not yet. – Matthew 24:6

> And this gospel of the kingdom will be preached in all the world as a witness to all the nations, and then the end will come. – Matthew 24:14

The Signs of the Time of the End

Following the Eighth Sign, Jesus continued in the Olivet Discourse to give an additional group of signs, which apply to the time of the end. Upon the fulfillment of the pivotal sign (the Gospel preached to the whole world), Jesus said the end will come. In my understanding, the "end" of which Jesus spoke can be identified as the Time of the End, a brief but intense period of history which ends the present age.

Most premillennial scholars believe that the end time, starting with the Tribulation, will begin with the Rapture. There are others who think that the Rapture will occur about three and one-half years after the beginning of the Tribulation. All agree upon a series of terrible judgments which will immediately precede the glorious Second Coming, and they refer to that series of events as the End Time.

At what point in this sequence will the Rapture happen? I believe that in this list of signs, the Rapture would occur immediately after the Eighth sign and before the final group of signs. On an appointed day, the Lord will descend from Heaven to receive His victorious Church. Not to rescue a decimated and defeated group hiding in the hills, but to receive a victorious Church which has overcome and occupied. This is the Church possessing the spirit expressed in the words of the old hymn, "The Kingdom is Coming."

> The sunlight is glancing o'er the armies advancing, to conquer the kingdoms of sin;
>
> Our Lord shall possess them, His presence shall bless them, His beauty shall enter them in.
>
> The kingdom is coming, O tell ye the story, God's banner exalted shall be! The earth shall be full of His knowledge and glory, As waters that cover the sea![1]

This is the Church that captures the concept of conquest. It may no longer sing "Onward Christian Soldiers," but it still embraces the attitude of advance, not retreat. The Church for which Jesus returns would still agree with hymn writer Sabine Baring-Gould, who penned the following words.

> Onward, Christian soldiers, marching as to war, with

> the cross of Jesus going on before! Christ, the royal Master, leads against the foe; forward into battle, see His banners go!
>
> Onward Christian soldiers, marching as to war, with the cross of Jesus going on before! At the sign of triumph, Satan's host doth flee; on, then, Christian soldiers, on to victory!
>
> Hell's foundations quiver at the shout of praise; brothers, lift your voices, loud your anthems raise! Onward, Christian soldiers, marching as to war, with the cross of Jesus, going on before![2]

When He comes, He will find that Church. And in it, He will find you! What will that moment be like? How can mere words describe it? Some glimpses in the scriptures ignite our imaginations. A great light will appear in the eastern sky. Jesus will appear in the clouds amid a fanfare by a loud trumpet and accompanied by angels. He will be shining like the sun, and speaking in a loud voice. He spoke in a loud voice at the tomb of Lazarus. Then, He merely said, "Lazarus, come forth!"[3] Perhaps in the Rapture, each believer will hear Him say in a loud voice, "Come Home!" The dead in Christ will rise instantly in their immortal resurrection bodies, and in the same instant, we who are alive will be transformed into our immortal resurrection bodies, and we all will be caught up to be with the Lord in the air! This will be the removal of the Church from Earth, just as the Tribulation Period begins. Later in this book, we will study what the Bible has to say about this blessed hope of every believer.

The period which follows the Rapture (the time which I refer to as the Time of the End) includes the time of Great Tribulation. How is this Time of the End period to be recognized? From Matthew, Mark and Luke we gain several more signs from the Olivet Discourse. Additionally we learn from the writings of the Apostle Paul that the Second Coming will not happen until two more signs appear: a great apostasy and the Man of Sin being revealed.[4] So, I have added those two signs to this period. With these, we can identify a total of twelve end-time events described in the New Testament. These are signs which begin with the abomination of desolation and continue through the Tribulation Period, up until the glorious Return of the Lord at the end of the age. Let's discuss each one in the following order.

- Abomination of Desolation
- Great Tribulation
- Apostasy
- Appearance of Antichrist
- Pestilences
- Fearful Sights in the Sky
- Distress of Nations
- Sea Waves Roaring
- The Sign of Jerusalem
- Sun and Moon Darkened
- Stars Falling
- Powers of Heavens Shaken

The Time of Great Tribulation

First in the second group of signs, the Abomination of Desolation will be seen in the temple at Jerusalem. This event signals the onset of the swift succession of signs in the Olivet Discourse which belong to the Time of the End. It is the first thing which Jesus mentions after saying that "then the end will come." Some premillennial scholars say that when this event happens, only three and one-half years of the Tribulation period will remain before the glorious return of Jesus to start the Millennial Reign. This mention of the Abomination of Desolation, recorded by both Matthew and Mark, is a scriptural reference by Jesus to the prophecy of Daniel. When Daniel used this term, he was describing something so loathsome and repulsive to worshipers that they would avoid its location and leave it desolate, unoccupied and unattended. The term is used in Daniel 9:27, 11:31, and 12:11. He predicted that a king would defile the temple by placing something so abominable in it that worship would be caused to cease. The Jews thought that an event about 350 years after the time of Daniel fulfilled this prophecy. In 186 B.C., the Syrian king Antiochus Epiphanes erected in the Jerusalem temple an altar to the pagan god Jupiter Olympus and sacrificed a pig.[5] This was not the fulfillment, however, since Jesus spoke of it as a still future event as he spoke with the disciples on the Mount of Olives in A.D. 33.

Furthermore, since the temple was destroyed by the Romans in A.D. 70, it has never been rebuilt. For this prophecy to be yet fulfilled, the Jerusalem temple must first be rebuilt. Since Israel took possession of the temple area in the 1967 war, there has been much talk of a rebuilt temple. However, given the current political tensions between Israel and the Moslem world, World War III would be ignited by such an attempt. It could be done only under a strong international treaty, enforced by a powerful and neutral military presence. According to Daniel 9:27, it will be a treaty that guarantees peace for at least seven years; at a time when temple sacrifices can be resumed. Considering all that would be involved, one might think that it is impossible. Such a thing would be a true miracle. However, as anyone familiar with the record of all the miracles in the Bible knows, miracles do happen in the Middle East!

Next is the sign of the Great Tribulation. The signal that it has begun is the event in the temple which we have just described. As we have pointed out, there is currently no temple. Somehow, in the future, there will be. And there, the Antichrist will set up a statue of himself to be worshiped as God.[6] That will be the Abomination of Desolation. When that event occurs, Jesus says, "…then shall be great tribulation, such as has not been since the beginning of the world until this time, no, nor ever shall be."[7] The period to which Jesus refers is, by His own words, to be considered worse than anything that has ever happened in history. There will be a worldwide persecution of believers, culminating in an actual war led by Antichrist against the saints. In Revelation 7:9-14, a great multitude of saints of all nations, tribes, peoples and tongues is seen standing before the throne in Heaven, clothed in white robes, praising Jesus. John is told that these are the ones who come out of the Great Tribulation. Apparently, innumerable thousands will die for their faith in this period.

At the beginning of the Tribulation will appear another sign – one which Paul mentioned. It will be the great Apostasy (called in the NJKV "falling away;" and in the NIV, "rebellion.")[8] During this period, the apostate church will still be on earth. This church will be the visible organization of Christendom that will remain on Earth after the Rapture. It will be comprised of those who are not born-again, and for whom religion is only an outward form of godliness. It will unite with other false religions across the globe to form a great political action force which actually helps bring the Antichrist to power. The "falling away" or apostasy doubtless will gradually develop over a period of years before the Rapture. The increasingly political character of this last-days church structure, combined with a decreasing interest in the Person of Jesus Christ will make it recognizable to true Christians.

In the period shortly after the Rapture, the power of the apostate church will quickly accelerate. This will happen because the restraining power of the Holy Spirit against evil will be taken away, following the Rapture. It is not possible that the omnipresent Spirit will be absent, but during that perilous period, He will not restrain evil human ambitions in the sense that He does now, in the present age. With a new eloquence inspired by Satan, the false prophets will deceive great followings of people. Then the religions of the world will begin to redefine morality: they will call evil, "good," and call good, "evil." A new religious leader, adored all over the world, will lead the world to serve the Antichrist. This is the False Prophet of the Antichrist, who "speaks like a lamb but has horns like a dragon."[9] That phrase means that, although he really represents Satan and the Antichrist, this religious leader will speak like a devout Christian.

The Antichrist

This is not a "doom and gloom" book. There are many more exciting things to discuss here than the reign of the Antichrist. Yet, since the rise of the Antichrist will be one of the signs that we are near the Time of the End, we will give it a brief mention here and move on. According to Daniel 9:27, the Antichrist will come to power and establish a seven-year treaty with the Jewish people (Israel), and then in the midst of that period will turn on the Jews and reveal himself as their enemy. He will show himself also as the enemy of all who refuse to receive his "mark." This mark is mentioned in Revelation 13:16-18. It is the number 666. There are many theories about the construction of this number and its connection to the person of the Antichrist. However, a careful study of the larger context of the passage in Revelation shows that the number more likely applies to a worldwide system, rather than to one person. But of course the system will be under the control of the Antichrist. In that system, no one can buy or sell without receiving that mark. Imagine not being able to get money out of the bank, nor groceries to feed your family, nor medicine for a sick child, unless you have such a mark. But an angel of God in Revelation 14:9-11 warns you that if you receive the mark you will burn forever in Hell.

How will you recognize the mark of the beast (Antichrist)? With the promotion of this mark comes the requirement that you must worship an image (statue) of the Antichrist. The awful time called the Great Tribulation will ensue because this charismatic leader will have the popularity to change laws and religions; and then use his power to install a statue of himself as an object of worship in the Jewish temple. This will be the Abomination of Desolation which was foretold by Jesus, and the signal that the Great Tribulation has begun. According to Revelation 7:9-14, a great multitude will be saved and *martyred* during the Tribulation. Those who are not killed will resist worship of the Antichrist and will become targets of more intense persecution. But this will be a period of only 42 months, and at the end, Jesus will return with all the saints from Heaven and destroy the Antichrist with the brightness of his coming.

The next sign in this group is pestilences. Luke gives essentially the same list as Matthew, but he adds two things to this part of the list. Luke mentions "pestilences and fearful sights in the sky."[10] Here, pestilences are grouped with the other disasters and with one very different new element mentioned by Jesus: "fearful sights in the sky." The fearful events in the sky identify this final cycle of pestilences as a sign of the end. The real sign here is not the familiar occurrences of earthquakes, famines and pestilences. Regardless of how many times in history these will have already occurred, at the time of this sign, such disasters will be widespread and *concurrent* with fearful sights in the sky. The specific mention of pestilences in this connection indicates that at the time of the end there will be a terrible group of plagues. Pestilences like HIV/AIDS have devastated and impoverished whole nations already. One can only imagine what this reference to future pestilences may entail.

The sign of fearful sights in the sky is a new element in the list. Various scholars have guessed at what they might be. Could they be comets on collision courses toward Earth? Could it be the darkening of the sun's light or the darkening of the moon? Could it be that the earth's axis changes or that its rotation speeds up, so that the stars appear to be falling from the sky? It is also mentioned in the context of this verse that the powers of heaven will be shaken. Whatever they are, these signs will bring distress of nations. The word "distress" in Luke 21:25 is from *stenochoreo*, which is the kind of anguish produced from being forced into a very narrow place. This may be a hint that as the signs in the sky occur, the habitable parts of the earth will be greatly reduced. Just two verses earlier, in Luke 21:23, the word "distress" is translated from a different Greek word: *ananke*. This word denotes the anguish which comes from great necessity. This would be the case when there is overcrowding and loss of food supply.

Another sign in this group is the roaring of sea waves. Great tidal waves, monster storms and underwater tsunamis have all caused great devastation in coastal areas across the globe in recent years. In fact, many of these areas will not recover for years. But this specific prophecy of "the sea and waves roaring"[11] indicates that something even more fearful will threaten the whole earth, including all of its great port cities and centers of commerce. This threat is in addition to the fiery devastation which brings the end of Commercial Babylon, described in Revelation 18. There, the code name "Babylon" represents the worldwide system of trade. The great city which serves as its headquarters will be destroyed by fire, as indicated in Revelation 18:8-18; yet the destruction is described from the perspective of ships and sailors. The 2001 destruction of the World Trade Center could be a foreshadow of things to come. Whatever the cause of the fire in Revelation 18, the sea waves mentioned in Luke 21 will be an even greater source of terror and anguish.

The Sign of Jerusalem

Next in our list is the sign of Jerusalem surrounded by armies. "But when you see Jerusalem surrounded by armies, then know that its desolation is near."[12] "And Jerusalem will be trampled by Gentiles until the times of the Gentiles are fulfilled."[13] The situation of armies surrounding Jerusalem has been very common in the city's long existence. Jerusalem has been besieged and destroyed completely more than 20 times in known history. To understand this prophecy, we need to know that Jerusalem itself is a unique city in the plan of God. The city of Jerusalem figures largely in biblical literature. There is the historical Jerusalem, dating from before the time of Genesis 14. There is the Millennial Jerusalem, described by Ezekiel. Then there is the heavenly Jerusalem, which in the Book of Revelation approaches Earth from Heaven and seems to be suspended in space. Which Jerusalem? The disciples would have understood Jesus to be referring the historical city, which exists to this day.

Was Jesus referring to what was to happen just 40 years later, when Jerusalem was surrounded by Roman armies? Certainly, some aspects of this prediction by Jesus did occur in A.D. 70, when after a three-year siege, Roman forces were able to destroy the entire city. Yet, many other aspects which must accompany the fulfillment of this prophecy did not happen at that time. The end did not come in A.D. 70. For fulfillment of the prophecy, the end of the age would come and Jesus would return. So, the event to which Jesus referred has not yet happened. Many scholars do believe that the Roman destruction of the city started the prophetic age called the Times of the Gentiles. They count the destruction of Jerusalem in A.D. 70 as the beginning of the Gentile Period. However, the phrase "times of the Gentiles" could also be understood to refer to a still future period, when the Antichrist and his forces will be in charge of the holy city.

This particular sign of armies surrounding Jerusalem is in the context of several other end-time events, so we may conclude that Jerusalem will yet be surrounded by armies. These armies will likely not be just armies of Rome, but armies from all nations. That such an event will happen in the last days, just before the return of Jesus, is prophesied in Zechariah 14. It is also described, in detail, in Ezekiel 38 and 39.

We will deal with these prophesies later as we look at events leading up to the battle of Armageddon, which will end when Jesus comes in power and great glory.

The Collapse of the Solar System

The next signs in this last list are almost a separate group in themselves. Yet, the sun and moon darkened, stars falling, and the powers of heaven shaken, seem to be so closely related that they may be considered as one cataclysmic event. They could all be caused by a disruption of our entire solar system, or these phenomena might result only from some drastic change in the orbit or rotation of Earth. We must also keep in mind that the entire Olivet Discourse is delivered in the literary style which we call apocalyptic. The linking of these three light sources in apocalyptic literature indicates a collapse of the natural order of things in the sky. All of these things happening at once will cause hearts to fail. Heart failure, from sheer terror, will become the number one cause of death on the planet at that time! In Luke 21:26, The New International Version puts it this way: "Men will faint from terror, apprehensive of what is coming on the world, for the heavenly bodies will be shaken." The Living Bible says, "The courage of many people will falter because of the fearful fate they see coming upon the earth, for the stability of the very heavens will be broken up."

The prophet Haggai foresaw this as a prelude to the coming millennial reign of the Lord. "For thus says the LORD of hosts: 'Once more (it is a little while) I will shake heaven and earth, the sea and dry land; and I will shake all nations, and they shall come to the Desire of All Nations, and I will fill this temple with glory' says the LORD of hosts."[14] The writer of Hebrews commented on this prophecy and gave the following explanation. "Now this, 'Yet once more,' indicates the removal of those things that are being shaken, as of things that are made, that the things which cannot be shaken may remain."[15] These last signs also correspond to the opening of the sixth seal in the Book of Revelation. "I watched as he opened the sixth seal. There was a great earthquake. The sun turned black like sackcloth made of goat hair, the whole moon turned blood red, and the stars in the sky fell to earth, as late figs drop from a fig tree when shaken by a strong wind. The sky receded like a scroll, rolling up, and every mountain and island was removed from its place."[16] These cosmic catastrophes will end life on earth as we now know it. At that point, Jesus and all the saints will return from heaven and a new order will be established in the physical realm.

The Appearing of the Son of Man

At just this place in the discourse, Jesus transitioned from speaking of signs, to speaking of a sighting. The sighting will be Jesus, Himself. This event will be the reverse of the Ascension, and Jesus will stand again in the place from which He ascended, the Mount of Olives in Jerusalem. The signs we have just discussed will conclude the period called the Time of the End. After describing all of these, Jesus said, "At that time they will see the Son of Man coming in a cloud with power and great glory."[17] This will be the glorious return of the Lord in all his power, with the armies of Heaven. He will come to end the Battle of Armageddon and the siege of Jerusalem. Related passages are found in Psalms 2:1-2; Zechariah 14:3-4; and Revelation 19:11-16. I recommend that you pause here to read these descriptions of how Earth's final battle will end. His return will bring destruction to the Antichrist and his false prophet and all the armies that are fighting Israel. This enormous engagement will end the Tribulation Period, and initiate the beginning of the millennial reign of Christ. Our focus now, however, is the fact that Jesus predicts that His own glorious return will happen immediately after these last signs have been fulfilled.

We have now completed our overview of the Olivet Discourse by Jesus, along with some additional signs given in the writings of Paul. We have identified twenty or more signs of His coming and of the end of the age. We cannot claim absolute certainty about the order in which the signs of the Olivet Discourse will occur; nor exactly how they were understood by the first audience. We should remember that, as we study it in these modern times, we are significantly removed from the actual situation between Jesus and the four disciples. We must admit that we are removed in time, culture, language and mindset from the setting of that moment. Yet, the function of inspiration by the Holy Spirit works both in the writing and in the reading of Scripture. As we study these signs, the Lord through His Spirit is active in helping us know and understand what was meant. We have carefully noted other Scriptures alongside the accounts by the Synoptic writers, since the best commentary on any part of the Bible is the rest of the Bible. There is no substitute, especially in these latter days, for a thorough knowledge of the word of God.

In summary, the first group of eight signs precedes the coming of Jesus for the catching away of the Church. They all belong to the time Jesus referred to as the Beginning of Sorrows. The second group of twelve signs that we explored belong to the Time of the End, but precede the glorious return of Jesus. The final sign is the appearing of Jesus, coming in the clouds. These last signs depict events which almost certainly will take place near the end of the Tribulation Period. Is this list to be considered exhaustive, or are other signs mentioned elsewhere in the Bible? Actually, there are many other events associated with the "last days" in the Bible, which Jesus did not mention here. We will highlight several of these later. It was needful to begin with the Olivet Discourse, where we have the very words of Jesus. Not one word of His will ever fail to be accomplished. Upon that rock we can build all our hope.

ENDNOTES FOR CHAPTER FOUR

1. Mary B. C. Slade, "The Kingdom Is Coming," in *The Baptist Hymnal.* (Nashville: Convention Press, 1956), 409
2. Sabine Baring-Gould, "Onward Christian Soldiers," op. cit.
3. John 11:43b
4. Second Thessalonians 2:3
5. Merrill C. Tenney, ed. *Zondervan Pictorial Bible Dictionary.* (Grand Rapids: Zondervan, 1963), 5
6. Revelation 13:15; Daniel 11:37
7. Matthew 24:21 NKJV
8. Second Thessalonians 2:3 KJV
9. Revelation 13:11
10. Luke 21:11
11. Luke 21:25c NKJV
12. Luke 21:20 NKJV
13. Luke 21:24c; Daniel 9:27; Daniel 12:7
14. Haggai 2:6-7 NKJV
15. Hebrews 12:27 NKJV
16. Revelation 6:12-14 NIV
17. Luke 21:27 NIV

Chapter Five

ISRAEL IN THE LAST DAYS

The Day of the Lord

THE QUESTION ABOUT the end of the age, which triggered the Olivet Discourse, did not just pop into the disciples' minds out of nowhere. They brought up the subject because it was well known to them. The end of the age theme appears frequently in Old Testament prophesies in various passages; expressed in such terms as the "latter days," "last days," "the end," or the "Day of the Lord." It usually refers to the end of human history.[1] The question was, "What will be the sign of your coming and of the end of the age?" In the subsequent discourse, Jesus provided a key framework by which all of the Bible's end-time events can be organized. We need to keep in mind that the term "end of the age" encompasses the entire time period of all of those events. We can now place other signs of the end time, mentioned elsewhere in the Bible, loosely into the framework of the two groups discussed in the previous chapter.

Of all the Old Testament terms applying to the end times, the Day of the Lord is the most comprehensive. In Old Testament prophecies, the Day of the Lord described something so catastrophic that it would bring an end to the present age of the world, much in the same magnitude of destruction as the Genesis Flood. Some examples can be found in Joel 2 and 3 or in Zechariah 14. In New Testament writings by Paul and Peter, examples can be found in First and Second Thessalonians and in Second Peter. In the New Testament, these references connect God's judgment of the world with the return of Jesus Christ at the end of the age. The terms such as "last days" or "time of the end," or the "Day of the Lord" were closely associated phrases. When seen in the context of descriptions of the Day of the Lord, or of the Messianic Age, they can be used almost interchangeably.

The nation of Israel figures prominently in the last days. The Hebrew prophets saw a future when God would intervene on behalf of Israel, but not for Israel alone. Contrary to the narrow, ethnocentric views of the future which were predicted by pagan seers in surrounding nations; Israel's prophets saw God acting on behalf of all people, all nations. They saw the Day of Yahweh bringing justice and peace for the whole world. Nevertheless, several major signs of the end of the age have to do specifically with the nation of Israel. In the following section, we will discuss the signs which relate mostly to Israel in the last days; signs which point, in a general way, to the season of the return of the Lord Jesus. Some significant signs are given in the following list. The last four will be treated separately in Chapter Six.

- The Restored Nation of Israel
- Exodus II from the North

- The Revival of the Hebrew language
- Israel as a Nation Receives Jesus as Messiah
- Agriculture
- Streams in the Desert
- Reforestation
- The Eastern Gate
- Israel's Neighbor Nations and Future Wars
- Jerusalem a Source of International Anxiety
- Invasion by Northern Coalition and Persia
- Invasion by Eastern Army of 200 Million

The Restored Nation of Israel

When I was ten years old, Israel became a nation. On May 14, 1948, through a radio broadcast originating from the Tel Aviv Museum, David Ben-Gurion read the Declaration of Independence of the State of Israel.[2] The young nation immediately faced an invasion by the armies of five Arab states and successfully waged a desperate and costly war for independence. Armistice agreements were signed with Egypt, Lebanon, Jordan and Syria the following year. The fifth Arab state, Iraq, withdrew its forces without signing an armistice agreement. Israel received membership in the United Nations in May of 1950. The rebirth of a sovereign nation in its homeland, after an absence of two thousand years, was one of the great miracles of history. It was also an astounding fulfillment of ancient Hebrew prophesies.

In the time of the prophet Isaiah, the Northern Kingdom (Israel) was destroyed in 722 B.C. and the people relocated into scattered parts of the Assyrian Empire. But Isaiah's own nation of Judah had not yet been destroyed and his people had not yet been scattered. Judah would not be conquered and scattered until 586 B.C. Amazingly, Isaiah foresaw the Babylonian conquest which would happen more than a century after his own time. In an astounding prophecy, he gave the name of Cyrus, the Persian king who would liberate his people from the Babylonian Captivity, approximately 150 years before Cyrus was born.

> Thus says the LORD, your Redeemer, and He who formed you from the womb: "I am the LORD, who makes all things, who stretches out the heavens all alone, who spreads abroad the earth by Myself; who frustrates the signs of the babblers, and drives diviners mad; who turns wise men backward, and makes their knowledge foolishness; who confirms the word of His servant, and performs the counsel of His messengers; who says to Jerusalem, 'You shall be inhabited,' to the cities of Judah, 'You shall be built,' and I will raise up her waste places; who says to the deep, 'Be dry! And I will dry up your rivers'; who says of Cyrus, 'He is My shepherd, and he shall perform all my pleasure, even saying to Jerusalem, "You shall be built," And to the temple, "Your foundation shall be laid."'"[3]

Imagine yourself to be the king of Persia, and imagine that you have just conquered Babylonia. A prophet reads to you a scripture written 150 years before your time which names *you* as the one who will liberate the Jews and send them back to rebuild Jerusalem and the temple. What would you do? Perhaps Cyrus was already impressed with the reputation of the Jewish prophets Jeremiah and Daniel. He knew Daniel and very likely knew about Jeremiah. Perhaps it was Daniel himself who called Isaiah's prophecy to the attention of Cyrus. The Bible is silent on the matter of how Cyrus came to his decision. What is a matter of historical record is that Cyrus proclaimed the edict which can be found in 2 Chronicles 36:23 and Ezra 1:2-4. Amazingly, an archaeological artifact called the Cyrus Cylinder has been unearthed. It contains the same words that are found in the two Bible passages. This cuneiform inscription was made in 538 B.C. by King Cyrus himself, and is a remarkable confirmation of the Bible story. The Jews then returned to the land of Judah, but only as a small remnant; to be governed as a small district of just one province among the 120 provinces of the great Persian Empire.

Isaiah was given vision by the Holy Spirit to look down the long corridors of the centuries, far beyond the return of the remnant, which would start in the year 538 B.C. He saw his scattered people returning a second time, in the last days – in the time of the Messiah. In Isaiah 11, after a remarkable description of the Messiah and His reign, we find the following statement referring to "that day" in verses 11 and 12. Note the phrase "second time." Please also note that this re-gathering includes the dispersed from the fallen nation of the northern ten tribes (Israel, which fell in Isaiah's time); as well those to be dispersed from the southern kingdom (Judah, which fell long after Isaiah's lifetime). Here is the "second time" passage.

> It shall come to pass in that day that the LORD shall set His hand again the second time to recover the remnant of His people who are left, from Assyria and Egypt, from Pathros and Cush, from Elam and

> Shinar, from Hamath and the islands of the sea. He will set up a banner for the nations, and will assemble the outcasts of Israel, and gather the dispersed of Judah from the four corners of the earth.[4]

This prophecy began its fulfillment on May 14, 1948, when Israel was re-established as a nation. Since then, almost 3 million Jewish immigrants have moved to Israel from the four corners of the earth. The term for Jews returning to their homeland is *aliyah* and the returnees are called *olim*. Today *olim* from more than 170 nations have been re-gathered from the Diaspora, or the Dispersion. The point here is that Isaiah's prophecy is being fulfilled in our time! This is one of the signs of the last days, very closely associated to the time of the millennial reign of Messiah. Israel has now been a restored nation for more than sixty years. Can it be much longer before the Lord returns?

There are things to which we are so accustomed that we no longer realize their significance. For those born after 1948, there has always been an Israel. But for me, this restored nation and this re-gathering of Jews from all over the world is tremendously impressive. To visit that country even once in your lifetime is to witness a miracle. To see all of its commercial centers, universities, agriculture, industries and scientific research centers, is to see something only God could do. In my own lifetime, I have seen this country emerge into a powerful nation. It has been my personal privilege to travel to modern Israel on more than 30 visits. As a young man, I participated in an archaeological dig at Beesheba. During the 1980's, I served on the consular staff of the Jerusalem-based International Christian Embassy. Over the years, I led dozens of Holy Land study tours. On these tours we visited the biblical towns that exist to this day in Israel

- such places as Bethlehem, Hebron, Nazareth, Jericho and Jerusalem. We saw the modern cities of Haifa and Tel Aviv, populated with Jews from all over the world. Israel returned to its own land in the latter days, just as Isaiah said.

Isaiah was not the only prophet entrusted with this revelation. A final re-gathering of Israel was mentioned by other biblical prophets as well. We have the additional collective witness of Amos, Zephaniah and Zechariah. Amos said the captives would be brought back, planted in the land, and never again would they be pulled away from the land.[5] Zephaniah says to Israel, "The King of Israel, the LORD, is in your midst; you shall see disaster no more."[6] "At that time I will bring you back, even at the time I gather you..."[7] Zechariah also proclaimed the Lord's message concerning that time: "Sing and rejoice, O daughter of Zion! For behold, I am coming and I will dwell in your midst," says the LORD.[8] "And the Lord will take possession of Judah as His inheritance in the Holy Land, and will again choose Jerusalem."[9] Surely, as we reflect upon the startling fulfillment of these ancient prophecies of Israel, we must acknowledge that we live now in an awesome prophetic era.

Exodus II from the North

Operation Mordecai Outcry, an early 1980's movement orchestrated worldwide by the International Christian Embassy, staged protest demonstrations against the Soviet Union on the steps of capital buildings of nations all over the world. The theme which was chanted by the demonstration groups was, "Let my people go!" The protest was on behalf of Soviet Jewry, which were the targets of heavy oppression inside the Soviet Union. At the time, anti-Semitism raged and rampaged in Russian society. Jews were the objects of discrimination in the job place, in schools, and in courts. Those who applied for exit visas to immigrate to Israel were especially targeted. They were required to pay the equivalent of $3000 US dollars for the exit visa and to submit endless paperwork. At the same time, they lost their jobs and became pariahs in society.

Eventually, Mikhail Gorbachev relaxed the restrictions under a new policy called *glasnost*, and tens of thousands of Jewish immigrants crossed the borders into Eastern Europe, with no money and no possessions. Various private organizations provided busses to key airports, where these organizations had chartered flights to Israel waiting. By the end of the 1980's, 850,000 Soviet Jews made their way to Israel. After the breakup of the Soviet Union, over 1 million more Soviet Jews were settled in Israel.[10] Along with the tens of thousands of Jews emigrating per year from other European countries, this has amounted to an Exodus of biblical proportions.

Was this foreseen in the Bible? Does it have anything to do with the signs of the end of the age? Let's go back to a scripture written about 600 B.C., and see what Jeremiah the prophet says.

> Therefore behold, the days are coming," says the LORD, "that it shall no more be said, 'The LORD lives who brought up the children of Israel from Egypt,' "but, 'The LORD lives who brought up the children of Israel from the land of the north and from all the lands where He had driven them.' For I will bring them back into their land which I gave to their fathers.[11]

In modern times, we have witnessed a second Exodus from the

North, which is more impressive in size than the ancient one from Egypt. What could possibly be the explanation, other than a supernatural fulfillment of biblical prophecy? When it became a full-blown movement and millions of Jews were coming out of Russia, it received little attention in the Western press. However, much ado was made of this massive Jewish movement in Arab newspapers. In U.S. and European news media, this modern Exodus has been almost unnoticed. Still, another great prophecy of the Bible concerning the last days has been fulfilled. The prophetic clock seems to be moving more swiftly with each passing day!

The Revival of the Hebrew Language

For several centuries prior to the late nineteenth century, Hebrew was, in a practical sense, a dead language. Jewish communities around the world assimilated, as best they could, into their host societies; and spoke the languages of the nations in which they lived. Biblical Hebrew was learned and taught only by scholars, in connection with religious studies, or with recitations in the synagogues. The modern revival of Hebrew has been another amazing fulfillment of prophecy. The revival of the language as a mother tongue for Israel began in 1882, with the immigration of Eliezer Ben Yehuda to Israel (known as Palestine at that time). It is an inspiring story.

Ben Yehuda determined that his family would speak only Hebrew at home. He started a movement of schools for children among the *kibbutzim* scattered throughout Palestine.[12] The language used in the schools was Hebrew. He dedicated himself to a life-long task of producing a Hebrew dictionary. Other Jews in Eastern Europe were inspired by Ben Yehuda's example and moved to Israel to join his movement. The result was that soon, all native-born Jews in Israel (called *sabras*) grew up with Hebrew as their mother tongue. When Israel declared independence and was fully recognized as a sovereign state, it had its own national language. Hebrew was alive again!

Founded upon the work of Ben Yehuda, today a National Academy of Language in Israel serves to prevent the pure Hebrew language from becoming polluted with borrowed terms from other languages. When new vocabulary words are needed because of modern inventions, a suitable word is found in biblical Hebrew. It is significant that you cannot speak Hebrew while uttering profanity. When an Israeli curses, the words must be borrowed from other languages. Even as early as in Zephaniah's day, the spoken Hebrew had been so influenced by other languages that it had changed into a different dialect than the Hebrew spoken by the Patriarchs. But Zephaniah predicted the restoration of a pure language in the last days.

The prophet Zephaniah foresaw the future gathering of the people back into the land. He also saw a time when their language would be revived. He said, "For then I will restore to the peoples a pure language, that they all may call upon the name of the LORD, to serve Him with one accord."[13] What makes this fulfillment of prophecy an even greater miracle is that, not only is the language alive again, but it is a pure language. Hebrew is the language of government, education and commerce in Israel today. Today, Hebrew language newspapers and magazines can be found on newsstands throughout the world. Israeli films and music are produced in Hebrew and are enjoyed by people in every part of the globe. But there is an even greater use of the restored language – yet to come. According to Zephaniah's prediction, the re-gathered people will all call upon the name of the Lord in one accord!

Israel as a Nation Receives Jesus as Messiah

Part of Zephaniah's prophecy about the restored language has to do with "calling upon the name of the Lord." The purpose of the revived language, in God's plan, has much to do with turning His ancient people back to Him and uniting their hearts in worship. Israel has been gathered again as a nation, but relatively few Jews in Israel have received Jesus as Messiah. Today, in Israel there are many Jews who are Jewish in culture and ethnicity only. They are completely secular and do not observe *Shabbat* or keep *Kosher*. Besides these, there are dozens of denominations and sects within Judaism. Their religious life is divided, even though they exist together in a Jewish state.

Among these groups is the Reformed denomination of Judaism, which is the most liberal branch. They support full participation of gays and lesbians in the synagogue and in social life. Other Jews in Israel belong to *Masorti* Judaism (Conservative). They observe *Shabbat*, practice *Kashrut* (keeping Kosher) and consider biblical principles to be normative for daily life. There is also a smaller but more vocal and politically powerful group, the Orthodox, who hold to strict observance of traditional ceremonies and festivals and do not recognize other Jewish groups. Then there are the *Heredi* Jews who sometimes are called "Ultra-Orthodox." Among them are the *Hassidim,* who are considered religious extremists, even by other Israelis. They embrace the Kabbalah as scripture and allow the decisions of their spiritual leader (called a *rebbe*, or *tzaddik*), to be authoritative over such personal choices as when to buy a house or whom to marry. There are at least a dozen other smaller sects of Judaism in Israel. In the last days, all these fractions will be united in their worship of Jesus as *Yeshua ha Meshiach*! Today, there are congregations of Messianic believers scattered throughout Israel, and their number is growing. According to Zephaniah, all of these groups will join one day in calling upon the name of the Lord together!

"*Baruch habah bashem Yahweh*" (Blessed is he who comes in the name of Jehovah). This four-word Hebrew expression is from the last sentence of Matthew 23:39. Speaking to the religious leaders of Jerusalem, Jesus said, "For I say to you, you shall see Me no more till you say, "*Blessed is He who comes in the name of the LORD!*" According to the Bible, shortly before the return of Christ there will be a time when Israel as a nation will receive Jesus as Lord; or as the Messianic Jews refer to Him, *Yeshua ha Meshiach*. This is according to the uniform teaching of Jesus, Peter, and Paul. Jesus will return to Jerusalem only when its inhabitants are ready to welcome Him and say, "Blessed is He who comes in the name of the LORD."[14] The conversion of Israel is prophesied by Peter in Acts 3:19- 21; where the arrival of "seasons of refreshing" and "times of restoration of all things" is dependent upon the sending of the Christ to Israel at the end of the age.

Conversion to Christ is not merely an acknowledgement of who He is. Ezekiel, prophesying in about 590 B.C., looked ahead through the centuries and saw Israel with a new heart. He predicted a time when Israel would be restored to her land and be given a new heart and a new spirit. "I will give you a new heart and put a new spirit within you; I will take the heart of stone out of your flesh and give you a heart of flesh. I will put My Spirit within you and cause you to walk in My statutes, and you will keep My judgments and do them."[15] When seen in the context of other prophecies of the end-time conversion of Israel as a nation, Ezekiel's prophecy almost certainly should be understood to refer to the same thing.

In other prophecy, it is made clear that this new heart and new spirit follows repentance and forgiveness. In an eschatological section of the book which bears his name, the prophet Zechariah predicts a second re-gathering of Judah and Israel. Keep in mind that he is prophesying in Jerusalem *after* the time of the first return of Jews from the Babylonian captivity. He says, of a future time, "I will sow them among the peoples, and they shall remember Me in far countries; they shall live, together with their children, and they shall return."[16] Following that, he says, "It shall be in that day that I will seek to destroy all the nations that come against Jerusalem. And I will pour on the house of David and on the inhabitants of Jerusalem the Spirit of grace and supplication; then they will look on Me whom they have pierced…"[17] A fountain of forgiveness will be opened for Israel as they look to Jesus and pray. The appearance of Jesus will bring the repentance and conversion and the blotting out of the sins of Israel.

The blotting out of sins is mentioned by Paul in Romans 11, where he explains that Israel's unbelief is dealt with in two ways: (1) even now, there is among Israel "a remnant according to the election of grace."[18] This refers to Jews who were being converted to Jesus in the time of Paul, and of course to all those converted since that time, and to those who are being converted now as the Gentile age continues. (2) In the future there will be a comprehensive conversion of Israel. This is because God made a covenant promise to them. Paul tells us,

> "For I do not desire, brethren, that you should be ignorant of this mystery, lest you should be wise in your own opinion, that hardening has in part happened to Israel until the fullness of the Gentiles has come in. And so all Israel will be saved, as it is

> written: 'The Deliverer will come out of Zion, and He will turn away ungodliness from Jacob; For this is My covenant with them, when I take away their sins.'"[19]

The apostle, writing under the inspiration of the Spirit to the Roman Christians, is quoting from a Messianic passage in Isaiah which says "And it will be said in that day: 'Behold, this is our God; we have waited for Him; we will be glad and rejoice in His salvation."[20] God will keep His promise to Abraham. God called Abraham and promised that through him, and in his seed, all the nations of the earth should be blessed.[21] The strange preservation of the Jews through so many centuries as a distinct people would be inexplicable apart from a divine plan. It is amazing to see what God is doing with Israel in our time, as well as exciting to anticipate the Messianic awakening which is yet to come.

Agriculture

Israel today is about 1/8 the size of Georgia in the U.S. Much of its territory is mountainous or desert. In fact, it is one-half desert. That makes Israel's agricultural production and prosperity even more surprising. This tiny nation's varied topographical, climatic, and soil conditions allow it to grow a wide range of agricultural produce. Israel's limited land space ranges from sub-tropical to arid, from 1300 feet below sea level to 3300 feet above sea level, and from sand dunes to heavy alluvial soils. Most Israelis will say that their success in agriculture comes from determination and ingenuity on the part of both the farming and scientific communities, which have partnered to develop a flourishing agro-business industry in the face of so many adverse soil conditions. While this is true, there is a higher reason for Israel's agricultural success. According to the Bible, God planned in the last days to demonstrate His blessings by causing the land to be abundantly fruitful.

Isaiah is speaking of the time of the Messiah when he says, "Until the spirit be poured upon us from on high; then will the steppe become garden land, and the garden land be counted an orchard."[22] Also, "The desert and the parched land will be glad; the wilderness will rejoice and blossom."[23] In Isaiah 27, the phrase "In that day" occurs four times, clearly identifying that the future period being described in the chapter is associated with the end time. In verse 6, the prophet says, "In days to come Jacob will take root, Israel will bud and blossom and fill all the world with fruit."[24] Some theologians think of these references only as metaphors. They are not only metaphors of God's blessing; they are also tangible evidences of it. Among the first products from Israel to be marketed in U.S. groceries were the Jerusalem artichoke and the Jaffa orange. In recent years, several new crops, "notably tomatoes and melons, have been adapted for growth in the desert with saline water irrigation. These are marketed under the brand name "Desert Sweet.'"[25] Today, supermarkets in Europe, Asia and the United States offer a variety of Israeli-grown fruit – much of it from the desert.

When European Jews began resettling their historic homeland in the late 19th century, they bought land from the Arabs who had lived in Palestine for the last several centuries. The land, which was mostly undesirable, was sold to the Jews at premium prices. Determined settlers began the work of reclaiming swamps, semi-arid land, hill land which had been ruined by deforestation, soil erosion and neglect.[26] I remember an Israeli settler telling me that the additional cost of reclaiming the land after purchase averaged about $5,000 per acre. Today, Israel is leading the world in agricultural expertise. Agricultural projects and research collaboration constitute about half of Israel's international cooperation programs. Emphasis is placed on training courses in agricultural subjects, with some 1,400 participants from over 80 countries attending specialized courses in Israel every year, and thousands of trainees receiving on-the-spot training in their own countries. Since 1958, thousands of Israeli agricultural experts have been sent abroad on long- and short-term assignments.[27]

It is especially interesting that the word "blossom" was used repeatedly in the predictions of a latter day fruitfulness of the land. Israel is one of the world's leading exporters of flowers. Using hi-tech innovation and ingenious irrigation schemes, Israel makes up for lack of water and capitalizes on its long sunlit days to produce flowers in abundance even in winter, in time for Valentine's Day in Europe. The flowers are cut and shipped by plane overnight to European countries – even Holland, which is known for its flowers. Profits of the Israeli flower market in Israel on Valentine's Day alone total approximately 2 ½ million dollars annually.[28] In our time, Israel's parched land is blossoming.

Amos spoke specifically of agricultural prosperity in his prophecy dated about 755 B.C. He looked past the coming destruction of the northern kingdom of Israel to the time of its restoration as a nation; when it would permanently repossess the land. He was enabled by God to see across 2600 years to the restoration of Israel which began in 1948. He foresaw a time of rich productivity.

> "Behold, the days are coming," says the LORD, when the plowman shall overtake the reaper, and the

> treader of grapes him who sows seed; the mountains shall drip with sweet wine, and all the hills shall flow with it. I will bring back the captives of My people Israel; they shall plant vineyards and drink wine from them; they shall also make gardens and eat fruit from them." I will plant them in their land, and no longer shall they be pulled up from the land I have given them," says the LORD your God.[29]

Ezekiel also saw this future time when God would restore the nation to its once-desolated homeland.[30] He prophesied that it would come when God cleansed the people from all their iniquities, so this prophecy can only be completely fulfilled when Israel receives forgiveness and accepts Jesus as the Messiah who atoned for their sins. In that future period, Israel's crops would never fail; famine would never come.

> "I will deliver you from all your uncleannesses, I will call for the grain and multiply it, and bring no famine upon you. And I will multiply the fruit of your trees and the increase of your fields, so that you need never again bear the reproach of famine among the nations."[31]

Ezekiel predicted that the desolate land would become like the Garden of Eden. "The desolate land shall be tilled instead of lying desolate in the sight of all who pass by. So they will says, 'This land that was desolate has become like the Garden of Eden; and the wasted, desolate, and ruined cities are now fortified and inhabited.'"[32]

Streams in the Desert

In 1969 I worked in an archaeological excavation project near Beersheba in the Negev. All that summer, we camped in desert terrain. The entire horizon was the color of sand, because sand was all that could be seen in any direction. From 9 AM until 4 PM daily, the sky was the same color, because it too was filled with sand – blown by the desert wind. I returned to the dig site just five years later, in 1974, to see a far different landscape. The horizon was green, checked with great patches of red and yellow. The land was covered with flower farms growing tulips, crocuses and other flowers.

How could the land be transformed from a barren, beige desert to a fruitful, flower-covered field so quickly? In recent years, much of the desert has been reclaimed with the help of a great underground water reservoir discovered in part of the Negev. The underground water is under such pressure that in many locations it does not need to be pumped. Once well-holes are drilled, water is pushed upward by underground pressure and flows into irrigation systems. It is not hard for me to imagine how quickly the entire landscape of Israel will change; as the Lord Himself prepares the land for His coming.

Israel's Reforestation

If only Mark Twain could see it now! The world's largest reforestation project is going on in the nation of Israel. It is also called "aforestation," since it involves growing trees on land which had no history of trees at all. The land has been barren and desolate for centuries. When Mark Twain visited in 1867, he described a dismal landscape that was all rocks and weeds – no trees to be seen anywhere. Hills that once were covered with orchards and olive groves had been desolated since the time of the Ottoman Empire's 400 years of rule which ended in 1917. It seems that the Turkish regime demanded from landowners certain taxes which were based upon the number of trees on the land. Naturally, the landowners responded by cutting down their own trees.

Under the administration of the Jewish National Fund (JNF), millions of trees have been planted in the past 60 years. One of the long-term projects of the JNF around the world has been raising funds for planting trees. When I traveled across the U.S. Southeast in the mid-eighties on behalf of the International Christian Embassy, we held "Bless Israel" rallies in the churches. In those rallies, churches gave offerings to bless Israel's land by planting trees. The funds were turned over to the JNF, and thousands of trees were planted. Synagogues and Jewish agencies around the world have used the famous "blue boxes" to collect funds for JNF for decades. In Israel, JNF operates tree nurseries and assists with the development of Israel's national forests. Over three million seedlings are planted in Israel per year. The seedlings have now grown into huge forests which blanket the hills and mountainsides. So many trees have been planted that the climate has subtly changed, so that parts of Israel now receive summer rains, mentioned in the Bible, but long absent. The trees provide windbreaks and cut down on wind erosion, as well as improving air quality by providing a source of oxygen.

Isaiah prophesied of a time when the Lord would restore Israel to the land, when the wastelands would be covered with trees, and even mentions the species of trees by name.

> I will make rivers flow on barren heights, and springs

> within the valleys. I will turn the desert into pools of water, and the parched ground into springs. I will put in the desert the cedar and acacia, the myrtle and the olive. I will set pines in the wasteland, the fir and the cypress together.[33]

Note that this prophecy is set in a large section which describes, from Isaiah's perspective, the distant future. The land has had no such renewal since Isaiah's day. The particular trees named in that prophecy are now being planted in the desert wastelands: Cedar, Acacia, Myrtle, Olive, Fir, and Cypress. Some of them are trees donated by my Jewish friends in honor of my recovery from a serious illness. In fact, in front of a grove of 200 trees on Mount Devorah in Galilee, there is a marker which bears the names of Doug and Jackie Chatham. On many occasions, my wife and I have participated in tree planting ceremonies at several planting sites in Israel. I believe that what we are seeing in Israel today is a significant sign that we are in the prophetic era of the last days.

The Eastern Gate

One of the most beautiful photographic views in Jerusalem is the Golden Gate, seen through the olive and palm trees of the Garden of Gethsemane. Seeing the large double tower bathed in the golden hue of the morning sun, one senses some special connection between this silent sentinel and splendor yet to come. Indeed, in the past three thousand years, it has witnessed great things. It was through this gate that Jesus made His triumphal entry into Jerusalem on Palm Sunday. It was once known as the Beautiful Gate and saw the healing of the lame man (Acts 3). It is also called the Eastern Gate, since it faces the East. Through this gate in the year A.D. 629 the Emperor Heraclius entered the city bearing what he regarded as the true Cross, which he had recaptured from the Persians. During the time of the Crusaders, the gate was opened only twice a year: on Palm Sunday and on the Feast of the Exaltation of the Holy Cross. The present form of the gate was given during the time of Justinian, although the foundations go back to the time of Solomon. It was built into the present city wall in A.D. 1540 by the Moslem ruler, Suleiman the Magnificent.

In the year A.D. 1530, just ten years before the gate was incorporated into the present city wall, it was permanently sealed by the masonry construction which is visible today. The Moslems did this because a prophecy in Ezekiel 44:3 had been called to their attention. According to their understanding, a conquering Jewish ruler would come through that gate. To prevent this, the gate was walled up. The Moslems might have read the verse which preceded the prophecy a bit more carefully. The exact wording of the prophecy also states that the gate will be shut and not opened. It will be reserved for none but the prince (the Messiah). Even their action of walling the gate shut was included in the prophecy. Remarkably, the gate has remained shut to this day.

This Golden Gate is the Eastern Gate which will indeed welcome the Lord Jesus at His glorious return in the Second Coming. He will arrive and stand first on the exact spot from which He ascended, on the Mount of Olives. This mountain is located directly across from the Golden Gate, on the eastern horizon. Jesus will proceed to take his rightful place on the throne of David on Mount Zion, within the walls of old Jerusalem, having passed through the Golden Gate. How fitting are the words of Psalm 24:7. "Lift up your heads, O you gates; be lifted up, you ancient doors; that the King of Glory may come in."[34] One of the signs of the times is this gate in old Jerusalem – exclusively reserved and waiting for the entrance of King Jesus!

ENDNOTES FOR CHAPTER FIVE

---

1. Leland Ryken, James C. Wilhoit, Tremper Longman III, eds. *Dictionary of Biblical Imagery.* (Downers Grove, IL: InterVarsity Press, 1998), 231
2. Howard M. Sachar, *A History of Israel From the Rise of Zionism to our Time.* (New York: Alfred A Knopf, Inc., 2001), 311
3. Isaiah 44:24-28
4. Isaiah 11:11-12
5. Amos 9:14-15
6. Zephaniah 3:15b
7. Zephaniah 3:20a
8. Zechariah 2:10
9. Zechariah 2:12
10. http://en.wikipedia.org/wiki/Aliyah, "Aliyah from the Soviet Union and post-Soviet States."
11. Jeremiah 16:14-15
12. Howard M. Sachar, A History of Israel from the Rise of Zionism to our Time. (New York: Alfred A. Knopf, Inc., 1996) 82-83
13. Zephaniah 3:9
14. Matthew 23:39; Luke 13:35
15. Ezekiel 36:26-27
16. Zechariah 10:9
17. Zechariah 11:9-10a
18. Romans 11:5
19. Romans 11:25-27
20. Isaiah 25:9
21. Genesis 12:3
22. Isaiah 32:15 SMITH
23. Isaiah 35:1 NIV
24. Isaiah 27:6 NIV
25. Jon Fedler, "Israel's Agriculture in the 21st Century." http://www.mfa.gov.il/MFA/Facts, Nov. 11, 2008
26. Ibid.
27. Ibid.
28. Nurit Felter, "Israel to Export 125 Million Flowers to Europe." http:www.ynetnews.com/articles, Jan. 31, 2007
29. Amos 9:13-15
30. Ezekiel 36:24
31. Ezekiel 36:29-30
32. Ezekiel 36:34-35
33. Isaiah 41:18-19 NIV
34. Psalms 24:7 NIV

Chapter Six

ISRAEL'S NEIGHBOR NATIONS AND FUTURE WARS

ISRAEL SELDOM MADE the front page of U.S. newspapers during the first decade of my ministry – during the years from 1957 until 1967. But in 1967, Israel fought its famous Six-Day War against overwhelming odds. It was then that they regained the old city of Jerusalem as their capital, and conquered the West Bank and Gaza. Until then, very few western nations saw any connection between the affairs of Israel and their own national security. That has changed in recent years – partly because of the volatility of the entire Mid-East region, and partly because Israel is a nuclear power. Speaking of the last days, the prophet Zechariah says,

> This is the word of the LORD concerning Israel. The LORD, who stretches out the heavens, who lays the foundation of the earth, and who forms the spirit of man within him, declares: "I am going to make Jerusalem a cup that sends all the surrounding peoples reeling. Judah will be besieged as well as

> Jerusalem. On that day, when all the nations of the earth are gathered against her, I will make Jerusalem an immovable rock for all the nations. All who try to move it will injure themselves."[1]

What does the Bible say about those surrounding peoples, or nations? In this chapter we will examine four more prophetic signs of the end of the age that involve the relationships of Israel with neighboring nations. They are:

- Israel's Relations with Neighbor Nations
- Jerusalem a Source of International Anxiety
- Invasion by Northern Coalition and Persia
- Invasion by Eastern Army of 200 Million

Israel's Relations with Neighbor Nations

Near the end of time, Middle-East nations with ancient names will again play key roles in world affairs. Although it is common for biblical prophecies to have both short-term and long-term fulfillments, there are several specific predictions concerning Israel and neighbor nations which have never been fulfilled. This is especially true of those which are connected with "Day of the Lord" or "in that day" prophecies. In several "in that day" prophecies, there are predictions that are completely improbable to people who are familiar with today's international politics. Let's start with Egypt. God, through the prophet Isaiah, tells us of a time "in that day" when Egypt will come to the Lord and be God's people! In fact, three nations: Egypt, Assyria and Israel will have an alliance and be a blessing to the earth! Read carefully the following prophecy:

> The LORD will strike Egypt with a plague; he will strike them and heal them. They will turn to the LORD, and he will respond to their pleas and heal them. In that day there will be a highway from Egypt to Assyria. The Assyrians will go to Egypt and the Egyptians will go to Assyria. The Egyptians and Assyrians will worship together. In that day Israel will be the third, along with Egypt and Assyria, a blessing on the earth. The LORD Almighty will bless them, saying, "Blessed be Egypt my people, Assyria my handiwork, and Israel my inheritance."[2]

There was a time in the mid-twentieth century that no Arab nation had peaceful relations with Israel. Thirteen Arab nations were in a state of declared war with Israel. Egypt became the first of these Arab nations to sign a peace treaty with Israel. On Saturday, November 19, 1977, President Anwar Sadat of Egypt stepped off a plane in Israel into a pivotal event in the turbulent history of the Middle East.[3] The next day was a day of destiny in which President Sadat addressed the Israeli Parliament and then personally talked with Prime Minister Menachem Begin about a path to peace between Egypt and Israel. Less than a year later in Washington, on September 17, 1978,[4] Sadat braved the opposition of almost all Arab nations, as well as the powerful Soviet Union; and signed the historic peace treaty with Prime Minister Begin.

Egypt's peace treaty with Israel has been a stunning surprise to the world! As the fulfillment of Isaiah's prophecy continues to unfold, we are likely to see two or three more amazing treaties in the Middle East. The next might be that the newly democratic nation of Iraq will make a treaty with Israel! Moslem Iraq and Jewish Israel? Highly improbable! Yet, the evangelizing of Iraq is happening now, quietly. Israel is also being prepared to receive Christ, quietly. Not today, but someday, this improbable alliance may be made. Iraq was once Assyria. Isaiah's prophecy mentions Assyria along with Egypt and Israel. Modern Iraq occupies a large part of the area of what was Assyria in the time of Isaiah. Not only Iraq, but other present-day neighbors of Israel would be included in this prophecy concerning Assyria. Jordan, Lebanon and Syria can also be included. At its zenith of power, Assyria's territory included all of these areas.

Today, Jordan is a modernized Arab nation, attempting to remain at peace with Israel after signing an armistice agreement at the end of the 1967 war. There is some likelihood that, in the near future, Jordan will make an alliance with Israel in the interest of economic and military stability. Some of the territory belonging to the former empire of Assyria lies in what are now the modern nations of Lebanon and Syria. Lebanon and Syria are hotbeds of Hezbollah aggression against Israel. Lebanon is essentially controlled by Syria. The probability that Syria will sign a peace treaty is remote; but actually no more remote than the probability, prior to 1977, that Egypt would make peace with Israel. Another war in the region might force the nations of Israel and Syria to the treaty table.

What's going to happen in the Middle East? No one really knows how God will work out the details, but we can be sure that Isaiah's prophecy will be fulfilled. Some parts of it are not hard to imagine. Israel and Iran will probably be at war. In fact, Iran is currently fighting a proxy war with Israel through Hamas in the Gaza Strip. When the conflict boils over and missile warfare breaks out between Iran and Israel, Jordan will be caught in the middle and will need

Israel's help. It seems credible that this could lead to a mutual-defense treaty with Israel.

Speaking in another prophecy, Isaiah says something else that seems relevant today regarding Gaza and Jordan. Set in the context of the second return of Israel to her land; and in a passage filled with descriptions of Messianic Age, a verse in Isaiah refers to expansions of Israel's control over neighbor nations. According to Isaiah 11:14, the expansion will include Philistia and the lands of Edom, Moab and Ammon. The Philistines in Isaiah's time occupied a coastland which included the present Gaza Strip. Ancient Edom, Moab and Ammon are all within the boundaries of Jordan today. In fact, the Jordanian capital of Amman is a modern spelling of Ammon. Here is the prophecy: "They will swoop down on the slopes of Philistia to the west; together they will plunder the people to the east; they will lay hands on Edom and Moab; and the Ammonites will be subject to them."[5] "The people to the east" may turn out to be Iran.

This prophecy refers to Israel near the end of this age, when a large area in the Middle East will either be occupied or protected by Israel. Even when taking into consideration Israel's military capabilities and her alliance with the West, this is an incredible scenario. Considering the combined might of all of the enemy nations and the arms which can be supplied to them by Russia or China, it will be a supernatural achievement. Yet, the Bible is a supernatural book and the prophecy of Isaiah must be taken as seriously as any other prophecy of the Bible.

The main point of the prophecy in Isaiah 19 concerning Israel, Egypt and Assyria is not how the three nations are united, but their common relationship to God. They will be together in their worship of God and in blessing the whole earth. Think of the tremendous shift in attitudes which will be required in all these nations! Today, like other Moslem states, Egypt, Syria, Jordan and Iraq follow the teaching of the Quran. The Quran teaches that Jews are the sons of monkeys and pigs.[6] Although Israel has Baha'i, Christian, Druze and Moslem minorities; it is officially a Jewish state. Most Israelis today would consider the notion of worshiping together with Moslems extremely ridiculous, if not blasphemous. Yet, the Word of God says that these nations will worship God together and be a blessing in the earth!

Other prophets in the Old Testament spoke of the future expansion of the nation of Israel. Zechariah, around 500 BC, spoke of a huge population in Israel in the end time. It will be so great that neighboring Lebanon and part of Jordan will be populated with Jewish people. "I will also bring them back from the land of Egypt, and gather them from Assyria. I will bring them into the land of Gilead and Lebanon, until no more room is found for them."[7] Ancient Gilead is part of Jordan today – the most fertile part, which is nearest to Israel. Ezekiel, about 600 BC, foresaw that in the end time the boundaries of Israel would be greater than ever before, even when ruled by David and Solomon. The boundaries would take in all of Lebanon and the lower half of Syria, as well as part of Jordan.[8]

Israel's long nightmare in history will have a happy ending. God has great plans for Israel in the last days. Although prophesies speak of the oppression of Jews by the Antichrist, of latter day invasions and of the last days battle of Armageddon; they also speak God's protection of Israel during the last days and the central role of Israel during the Messianic Age. Therefore, as we discuss the next few topics, we should see prophesies of future invasions in the greater context of prophesies of prosperity, expansion and blessing to the whole earth. As with all the rest of the world, God deals with nations season by season! Israel has gone through, and will go through, various prophetic seasons. It is sometimes difficult to precisely distinguish which prophecies will only be fulfilled in the Messianic Age; and which prophecies will be fulfilled quite soon, even before the time of the Tribulation. One thing is for certain: we should all be attentive to developments between Israel and her immediate neighbors. It is in that area of the world, more than in any other, that we should look for signs of His coming!

Jerusalem a Source of International Anxiety

Even the phrase, "the Middle East," has prophetic overtones. Thousands of years ago, God set Jerusalem in the midst of the earth. Located on a land bridge between three continents, it has become a holy city to three world religions. It is, in a very real sense, the key city in the Middle East. In the last days, it will be even more so. Zechariah prophesied that in the last days Jerusalem would become a "cup of trembling"[9] to the nations around her. The prophet goes on to say that the welfare of Jerusalem would become like a burdensome stone to all nations. This prophecy is found in Zechariah Chapter 12, a short chapter of only 14 verses; yet in that short passage the prophet repeats the term "in that day" no less than six times!

In previous centuries, very few nations at any given moment would have been concerned about Jerusalem. Today, however, that situation has been reversed. Now, the number of nations that are not concerned about decisions made in Jerusalem would be very few. Israel's seat of government is its parliament, called the Knesset, which is located in Jerusalem. Israel has dozens of political parties, and the Prime

Minister and Cabinet can hold office only as long as delicate alliances are maintained between various parties. This situation is a source of anxiety to world powers, since policy shifts occur frequently in Jerusalem. Moderate parties tend to attempt appeasement as the path to peace; conservative parties tend to take hard line stances, believing strength is the safest position from which to negotiate. Western powers worry. Whatever actions are taken by Jerusalem, they are sure to affect many nations.

Military leaders in many nations must now give great attention to the tensions between Jerusalem and other capitals in the Middle East. Today, several well-funded international terrorist organizations are dedicated to the complete destruction of Israel. Hezbollah in Lebanon and Syria, Hamas in the West Bank and Gaza, and other fundamental Islamic extremists carry out terrorist activities against Israel on an almost daily basis, and occasionally incite all-out war. Moreover, rogue nations threaten nuclear strikes. The ramifications of a shift in the balance of military power in the Middle East affect the entire world. The economies of many industrially developed nations are closely tied to Middle East oil supply. Whenever there are any flare-ups of military activity in the region, especially those involving Israel, those nations are deeply concerned with decisions made at the Knesset in Jerusalem. Each time there is a major incident involving Israel, ambassadors from the United States and other western nations urge restraint upon Israel's leaders, and their governments watch nervously to see what new decisions will be made by the Knesset or the Prime Minister in Jerusalem.

Jewish people all over the world turn their faces toward Jerusalem as they make their prayers. Jews and Christians throughout the world pray for the peace of Jerusalem, as instructed in Psalm 122.

This scripture tells us, "Pray for the peace of Jerusalem; 'May they prosper who love you. Peace be within your walls, prosperity within your palaces.' For the sake of my brethren and companions, I will now say, 'Peace be within you.' Because of the house of the LORD our God I will seek your good."[10] Today, there is an urgent need to pray for the peace of Jerusalem; as it exists under constant threat of destruction. The only true and lasting peace for the city will not be established until the Lord returns. Until then, Jerusalem will remain at the center-stage of world attention – another prophetic indication that we are in the last days before the return of Christ.

Invasion by Northern Coalition and Persia

Gog and Magog will in the last days send a great coalition of invading armies into Israel, according to the prophet Ezekiel. That prophecy is found in chapters 38 and 39 of Ezekiel. In the first two verses of chapter 38, the prophet identifies Gog as the prince or ruler of Rosh, Meshach, and Tubal. Magog refers to the land which he rules. Rosh is thought by some scholars to mean Russia; but others are uncertain. In traditional views, Meshach is thought to mean either Moscow; or a people called Moschi, spoken of in the Assyrian inscriptions as dwellers of the Caucasus mountain region.[11] Traditional scholars also believe that the name Tubal is associated with Tobolsk, a city in Siberia.

These identities are open for debate. Whatever their exact identity may be, however, Ezekiel describes their location as "the uttermost parts of the north." That would mean to the extreme north of Israel. Ezekiel is indicating nations beyond the Caucasus. On a map, one can easily see that the area described in Ezekiel's prophecy is known today as Russia. This does not necessarily mean, however, that this prophecy points only to the modern nation of Russia. It merely gives the location of the homeland of the invading force.

Some of the coalitions of nations which participate in this invasion are named in verse five of chapter 38. "Persia, Ethiopia, and Libya are with them, all of them with shield and helmet." We previously mentioned Syria and Egypt. What is amazing about these names of ancient nations and the name of Israel is that they long ago disappeared from the map; but in the last century they rose again, Phoenix-like, out of the ashes of the past. Egypt became an independent country in 1922; Syria in 1945, and Israel in 1948. Libya became a nation again in 1951. Persia is now called Iran. All these nations occupy essentially the same territory as they did in Bible days! These amazing developments comprise a noteworthy sign in themselves.

Verse 6 names two other groups: Gomer and Togarmah. Gomer was once a people group located north of the Caucasus, and Togarmah is likely a reference to Armenia. Again, these are traditional views which are opposed by some modern scholars. Regardless of to whom the names may refer, these lands are to the "far north" of Israel, and as such, are part of territory of the former Soviet Union. Again, this location is noted, not to make any prophetic claims about Russia; but simply to help the reader understand the geography as it would have been understood by Ezekiel's first audience.

The prophecy indicates that God will allow the invasion; in order to show Himself to the nations of the world through His dealing with Gog. "You will come up against My people Israel like a cloud, to cover the land. It will be in the latter days that I will bring you against My land, so that the nations may know Me, when I am hallowed in you, O Gog, before their eyes."[12] The invasion will fail, and most of the army will be destroyed in the mountains of Israel before it reaches Jerusalem. Ezekiel says that God will send a great earthquake, which will be felt even by the fish of the sea and the birds of the air - even insects – and "all men who are on the face of the earth." Something is being described here that is so powerful that it will have a worldwide impact. It will be much more than an ordinary earthquake: "And I will bring him to judgment with pestilence and bloodshed; I will rain down on him, on his troops, and on the many peoples who are with him, flooding rain, great hailstones, fire, and brimstone."[13]

Speculations about various kinds of chemical warfare, missiles and bombs cannot fully explain all of these effects in any natural ways. The main point here is that God will reveal Himself in this event; therefore these calamities will be supernatural and aimed only at the invading forces. In fact, Ezekiel goes on to say in chapter 39, verse six, that God will also, at the same time, retaliate by sending fire upon Gog's homeland, Magog. In summary, the invasion will fail and the homeland will be destroyed and God will be exalted as the protector of Israel. For seven months following, Israel will be occupied with gathering and burying the corpses of Gog's army. Search parties will set markers by each set of remains and other workers will carry them to a great burial place to be called Hamon-Gog, also to be known as Hamonah. Note this large number of specific details in Ezekiel's prediction. There will be little room for doubt when this great sign occurs.

In 2008, an alliance called the Shanghai Cooperation Organization held war games in western China and in the Ural Mountains of Russia. The participants included Russia, China and four central Asian republics which were formerly part of the Soviet Union.[14] It is also known that Iran has asked to join this alliance. We mention this here only as evidence that an alliance between Russia, Iran (Persia) and other nations to the north of Israel is possible. No one can say for certain when the army of Gog will be formed. However, when news headlines begin to speak of such an alliance, we should be aware that it is quite likely a fulfillment of Ezekiel's prophecy and a sign that end of the age is near.

Invasion by Eastern Army of 200 Million

Another sign, coming at the very end of the age, will be the gathering of armies from all nations in Israel. This will occur sometime after the northern invasion which we have just discussed. The final gathering of armies in Israel will begin with an invasion from the East, and this may be the pretext for the Antichrist to lead an international force from Europe into Israel. This will trigger the final war, which is mentioned in several passages in the Bible. The best-known passage is found in the Book of Revelation, which gives the actual size of the invading army: 200 million. Revelation chapter 9, verse 16 says, "Now the number of the army of the horsemen was two hundred million, and I heard the number of them".

Also found in the book of Revelation, along with the description of forces from the East coming to the world's last battle, is a given location: a place called Armageddon.[15] In the passage which names Armageddon as the battle site, Revelation states that the Euphrates River will be dried up in preparation for the invasion by the kings from the East. Fifty years ago, when I was a young minister, most scholars held the opinion that the huge number could not be taken literally. Never in history had a nation existed which could field an army so large. Today, of course, it is well known that the Peoples Republic of China claims an army of exactly that size. China lies to the east of Israel.

Armageddon means in Hebrew, "hill of Megiddo." It is the name of an ancient fortress site in northwestern Israel, not far from the modern city of Haifa. The hill overlooks the Valley of Jezreel, on the Plain of Esdraelon, leading from the seacoast into a great wide valley. The westernmost part of the valley, which is near Megiddo, is called the Valley of Megiddo. This narrow valley is the main passage through the Carmel mountain range. Once past the hill of Megiddo, the valley opens into a vast plain called the Plain of Megiddo. I have personally visited the extensive archaeological excavations there on numerous occasions. One can see at Megiddo today the ruins of the great fort built by Solomon. Points of interest include a unique interior water system, some massive 12 feet wide walls, ruins of stables for over 450 chariot horses, and a commanding view of the entire plain.

The fortified hill was located on the Via Maris, the coastal route which connected Egypt with Damascus. Megiddo's history as a site for major battles stretches back to the time of the Old Testament. Battles fought at this site involved Egyptians, Canaanites, Philistines, Israelites, Assyrians, Greeks, Romans, Persians, and British.[16] Solomon's fortress was built upon the accumulated ruins of perhaps 25 other forts which had occupied the same site for centuries.[17] In 609 B.C., Pharaoh Necho of Egypt marched by the site on his way to aid Assyria against the Babylonians, and was there confronted by King Josiah of Judah. King Josiah was killed after a brief skirmish. In 1799, Napoleon's army fought a battle at Megiddo; and he declared that it was an ideal place for strategic battles. Interestingly, one of Israel's most important military airfields is located near Megiddo today. It is today a strategic military target.

The battle which will be fought at Armageddon is to be the world's last battle before the return of the Lord and the end of the age. In Revelation, it is in the sixth bowl of wrath judgment, during the time of the final trumpet. Armageddon ends the Tribulation period and immediately precedes the final bowl judgment and the pronouncement from the throne in Heaven, "It is done!"[18] This is when every island will disappear and every mountain will be flattened in preparation for the Messianic Age. Although this passage is followed by two chapters which describe the fates of an ecclesiastical and a commercial Babylon, the next event in the chronology of Revelation is the glorious return of the King of Kings and Lord of Lords, described in chapter 19. That coming is timed so that it is the Lord Himself who ends the battle of Armageddon.

The destruction of the armies which had gathered for the battle, along with the capture of the Antichrist and his prophet, is described in Revelation 19.

> And I saw the beast, the kings of the earth, and their armies, gathered together to make war against Him who sat on the horse and against his army. Then the beast was captured, and with him the false prophet who worked signs in his presence, by which he deceived those who received the mark of the beast and those who worshiped his image. These two were cast alive into the lake of fire burning with brimstone.[19]

Additional information concerning this last battle is found in Revelation 13:20. That scripture indicates a blood-covered landscape that will extend around Armageddon to a distance of 1,600 furlongs, or about 184 miles. The distance includes the city of Jerusalem. This helps us understand how the battle zone could be so large that it could center both around Megiddo and Jerusalem.

Zechariah, speaking around 525 B.C., describes the same battle. He also links it with the coming of the Lord, who will end the battle and set up his millennial kingdom at that time. "For I will gather all the nations to battle against Jerusalem; the city shall be taken, the houses rifled, and the women ravished. Half of the city shall go into captivity, but the remnant of the people shall not be cut off from the city. Then the LORD will go forth and fight against those nations, as He fights in the day of battle."[20] The prophecy goes on to say that the Lord's feet will stand on the Mount of Olives and it will be split in two, making a large new valley, through which the refugees can flee to safety. During the day on which it happens there will be no light; but finally, in the evening there will be light. The method by which the armies are destroyed is like the effect of the nuclear blasts at Hiroshima and Nagasaki. "Their flesh shall dissolve while they stand on their feet, their eyes shall dissolve in their sockets, and their tongues shall dissolve in their mouths."[21]

This terrible devastation will not fall upon righteous people, but in fact, upon the most wicked people in all of history – those who would dare to fight against Jesus Himself when He comes to establish righteousness upon the earth! Another prophecy concerning this time, dating from around 1000 B.C., is found in Psalm 2. "Why do the nations rage, and the people plot a vain thing? The kings of the earth set themselves, and the rulers take counsel together, against the LORD and against His Anointed, saying, "Let us break their bonds in pieces and cast away their cords from us."[22] The collective military effort of the Antichrist and all the rulers on earth at that time will be directed against God and against Jesus Christ. They will try to destroy the city that Jesus intends to make His millennial headquarters. Then when they see Jesus coming, they will try to fight Him. Imagine trying to shoot Jesus out of the sky with missiles! Yet, millions today wish to throw off the rule of God in this world. They already have the same spirit.

ENDNOTES FOR CHAPTER SIX

1. Zechariah 12:1-3 NIV
2. Isaiah 19:22-25 NIV
3. Howard M. Sachar, *A History of Israel from the Rise of Zionism to Our Time.* (New York: Alfred A. Knopf, Inc., 1996), 847
4. Ibid, 854
5. Isaiah 11:14 NIV
6. *The Quran: Surah* 2:66, Surah 5:60 and Surah 7:166
7. Zechariah 10:10
8. Ezekiel 47:15-20
9. Zechariah 12:2 KJV
10. Psalm 122:6-9
11. Henry H. Halley, *Halley's Bible Handbook.* (Grand Rapids: Zondervan, 1965), 333
12. Ezekiel 38:16
13. Ezekiel 38:22
14. http://www.atlaspiers.com/dvd/dvd.html, 9/26/2008
15. Revelation 16:12-16
16. Neal W. May, *Israel a Biblical Tour of the Holy Land.* (Tulsa: Albury Publishing, 2000), 220
17. Ibid, 221.
18. Revelation 16:17
19. Revelation 19:19-20
20. Zechariah 14:2-3
21. Zechariah 14:12b
22. Psalms 2:1-3

Chapter Seven

SIGNS RELATING TO THE WORLD IN GENERAL

WHAT IN THE world is going on? And what does the Bible have to say about it? In Chapter Five and Chapter Six, we looked at signs of the end of the age which will be related to Israel as a nation. We turn our attention now to signs relating to the world in general. From many different prophecies found in the Bible, we can know quite a bit about the condition of the world at the end of the age. Descriptions of the end-time society fall into several categories, which we will explore in the order listed below. We believe that most of these will develop gradually, yet each movement can be considered as characteristic of the last days before the glorious return of the Lord Jesus. It might be that Christians will recognize these movements first as trends: trends to be expected to develop during the time preceding the Rapture. Following the Rapture, these movements will accelerate and reach their zenith during the period of the Tribulation.

- Spiritual Apostasy
- Flood of Evil

- Technological Development
- European Union
- World Revival of True Christianity
- World Religion Based on Astrology
- Environmental Crisis
- One-World Government

Spiritual Apostasy

The first of these end-time signs is apostasy, a falling away from the Church. It is possible that some major church denominations and organizations will end up as spiritually bankrupt systems. In the last days, ecclesiastical systems will be so influenced by humanism that they will lose all moral influence on the secular public. Secular humanism will be more popular than Christianity. The time near the end will be an age dominated by materialism. Many who continue to claim to be Christians will have a show of godliness, but deny its real effects. Self-indulgence, rather than sacrificial service, will be their lifestyle. Without moral leadership from the Church, society will spiral downward. From biblical descriptions of society in the last days, we know that five great sins will eat away at the moral core of social order; lawlessness will be the norm; and mind-controlling drugs will be used as a means of domination, perhaps even by governments. In this section we will identify prophecies which portray these conditions.

Writing to the Thessalonians, who were at the time going through intense persecution and were concerned that the Day of Christ had come, the apostle Paul said, "Let no man deceive you by any means;

for that Day won't come unless the falling away comes first, and the man of sin is revealed, the son of perdition, who opposes and exalts himself above all that is called God or that is worshiped, so that he sits as God in the temple of God , showing himself that he is God."[1] The expression "falling away" is rendered "rebellion" in the New International Version, and in other versions, "apostasy." Paul is saying that the Day of Christ will not come until the apostasy occurs and the Antichrist is revealed. How will the apostasy be recognized?

Explicit details are found in another of Paul's writings. Paul, shortly before martyrdom, was writing to Timothy concerning the last days. He said,

> But know this, that in the last days perilous times will come: for men will be lovers of themselves, lovers of money, boasters, proud, blasphemers, disobedient to parents, unthankful, unholy, unloving, unforgiving, slanderers, without self-control, brutal, despisers of good, traitors, headstrong, haughty, lovers of pleasure more than lovers of God, having a form of godliness but denying its power. And from such turn away![2]

This prophecy reads like today's headlines! It describes society in general very well. Yet it is intended to describe people who have fallen away from the church. They are not outsiders; they are "church people!" These are the ones who will have a "form of godliness" but will deny its power. These will have fallen away from Christ Himself while holding on to an outward profession of Christianity. The word "form" means outward appearance. In the last days, especially immediately prior to the Tribulation period, it will be easy to be considered a Christian, because no discipline, suffering or sacrifice is required. Perhaps this explains why, when persecution begins, the love of many will grow cold and why so many will fall away.

Jude reminds us that other apostles besides Paul spoke of the same apostasy which will come in the last days. "But you, beloved, remember the words which were spoken before by the apostles of our Lord Jesus Christ: how they told you that there would be mockers in the last time who would walk according to their own ungodly lusts. These are sensual persons, who cause divisions, not having the Spirit."[3] "Sensual" is used to describe those who live according to their own natural impulses. They are likely to cause divisions in congregations because they are not led by the Spirit of Christ. They are the ones who will resist spiritual leadership. They are "mockers" who don't believe that they are living in the last times; in fact, they mock the idea of a literal return of Christ.

Peter tells us that not only the apostles, but also the prophets, foretold that scoffers in the last days would turn away and live according to their own desires. "Knowing this first: that scoffers will come in the last days, walking according to their own lusts, and saying, 'Where is the promise of His coming? For since the fathers fell asleep, all things continue as they were from the beginning of creation.'"[4] Apparently, the Second Coming of Christ will not be a popular subject, even within the church community. At any rate, that belief will be rejected by the ones who have fallen away. One of the marks of the apostasy of which Paul and the other apostles spoke will be rejection of the doctrine of the Second Coming. Apostasy will set the stage for the Antichrist to deceive them. As Paul explains in Second Thessalonians, "And for this reason God will send them strong delusion, that they should believe a lie, that they all may be condemned who did not believe the truth but had pleasure in unrighteousness."[5]

All of us in Western society must exercise caution against allowing possessions to possess us. The end of the age will be marked by a world-wide materialistic system, so magnetic that it will even attract God's people. Possessions will seem more important than relationships. The world-wide commercial system is code-named "Babylon" in Revelation 18. It will be the basis of the world's political and financial power in the time of the Antichrist and the Tribulation Period, just before the Lord's return. As the system begins its development long before the Tribulation Period, God's people should heed the scriptural warning to come out of it and to separate themselves from it. "And I heard another voice from heaven saying, 'Come out of her, my people, lest you share in her sins, and lest you receive of her plagues.'"[6] There will be a point at which the cost of remaining in the system will be too great for all true believers. There may come a time, before the Rapture of the Church, in which participation in the world-wide system for buying and selling will require a costly compromise of Christian convictions.

Two antonymous interjections are conspicuous in the Revelation account of the prophesied destruction of the future world system in Revelation 18 and 19. They are "alas!" which means, "too bad!" and "alleluia!" which means, "praise God!" The double expression of "Alas, Alas!" appears in Revelation 18:10, 16 and 19 to underscore the lamentation over the absolute desolation of the world's mightiest commercial empire. This megalopolis of merchandise will not be the old Babylon restored, but a similar system that extends its political, economical, and ecclesiastical control world-wide. It will incorporate a world church, a world government, and a world trade system. Some scholars believe that it will be headquartered in Rome, which seems to be described in Revelation 17:9. Additionally, Rome is called

Babylon by Peter in First Peter 5:13, where he is clearly referring to Rome. When Babylon is destroyed, those whose hopes for happiness hinge on having worldly wealth will wail "Alas, Alas!"

But just beyond the "Alas!" of doomed Babylon lies the "Alleluia" of the saints whose stock will soar as Babylon smokes and sinks. Those whose treasure is in the currency of Heaven will survive the crash and praise the Lord. While those who have gained the world, but lost their souls, are crying "Alas!" there will be others, who have "lost" the world and gained their souls, that will be shouting "Alleluia!" They will be joyful because they will see that they made the right choice and Heaven has vindicated them. Missionary martyr Jim Elliot, who gave his life to reach the remote Aucas of Ecuador, said in his journal, "He is no fool who parts with what he cannot keep, to get what he shall not lose."

Flood of Evil

A flood of evil will sweep the earth in a tidal wave of filth and violence in the end-time. Five great sins will dominate the last-days society. According to Revelation 9, they will be idolatry, murders, drugs, fornication and theft.[7] Idolatry in the last days will include worship of demons and of actual handmade idols. The word "murder" in the Bible is usually understood to be intentional manslaughter, but does not include killing in wartime battle. The prevalence of murders in the last days will be comparable to the violence of the world in Noah's day. The word which is translated "sorceries" in Revelation 9:21 of the King James Version actually means "mind-controlling drugs." The widespread use of these drugs to deceive and enslave large populations is probable in the last days. Near the end, morality will be upside down: evil will be called good; good will be called evil. Sexual immorality will be socially accepted. However, in Revelation 9:21, "fornication" is a more precise translation than "sexual immorality," which is used in several modern versions. This particular sin has already greatly increased, partly from a breakdown in family values and partly from a huge sex slave industry.

Satan knows his time is short. He intended to extend and expand his evil empire, and Jesus is coming to end it. His demons are fanning winds of war to worry this weary world. Even now, Satan seeks to subjugate governments to unite them in rebellion against the coming of Christ. Whole nations such as Colombia and Mexico are sliding slowly into the clutches of drug cartels. Fundamentalist Islam dominates more than 50 nations now. Anti-Semitism, along its twin anti-Christianity, dominates society in many parts of Europe. Foreshadows of the Tribulation are already falling across whole nations, where spirits of Antichrist promote persecution of believers. Isaiah foretold this season in one of his prophesies concerning the coming of the Redeemer. "When the enemy comes in like a flood, the Spirit of the LORD will lift up a standard against him. 'The Redeemer will come to Zion, and to those who turn from transgression in Jacob,' says the Lord."[8]

The same flood of evil is described in symbolic language in Revelation 12. "So the serpent spewed water out of his mouth like a flood after the woman, that he might cause her to be carried away by the flood."[9] What will society be like when radio and television programming is no longer censored by Judeo-Christian standards? Nudity, sexual perversion, violent rapes and murders, filthy language and cursing will become the norm in regular daytime broadcasting. Bookstores and public libraries, electronic media and the Internet will be filled with evil material. Lack of moral restraint will result in danger to women and children, even in public places. Prejudice, bigotry, racial violence and "ethnic cleansing" will increase. Demonic possession will become common throughout the world, even in so-called civilized society.

Ironically, this flood of evil will be the occasion of the last great world-wide revival of the true Church. The Holy Spirit will empower believers to resist this tide of evil, and to overcome the devil by the blood of the Lamb and by the word of their testimony.[10] The Bible predicts a time when the Spirit of the Lord will lift up a battle standard against the enemy. There will be no difficulty in identifying the real Church among all the pseudo-churches. It will be active in witnessing and testifying to the reality of the Lord Jesus Christ and His saving power. Until the end of the world, supernatural signs and wonders will accompany the testimony of Jesus, and many will be saved, healed and delivered. As in all previous history when the Church goes through trial; true believers will separate themselves and overcome any temptation to blend into the ungodliness around them. This will give vitally needed credibility to their witness. The gospel of the Kingdom will be preached in all the world, as a witness to all nations. Only then will the end come, and not before!

Technological Development

The arrival of our technological age of computers, the worldwide web, cell phones, jet travel and space flight was surprising swift in the timescale of history. All of these technologies have developed during my own lifetime. It continues to surprise my younger friends that I grew up before plastic was invented. I saw some of the very first black-and-white television sets in use, and was a grown man before audio cassettes replaced the old flat phonograph discs. I sometimes feel like a pelican in a desert; far removed from my native culture, where I now teach via the internet and use a cell phone to talk to people in other countries. The current technological explosion didn't just happen by chance. I am convinced that each new technology merely builds upon laws of physics which God set in motion at the time of the Creation; and I am further persuaded that He controls the timing of their discovery. The sudden explosion of scientific achievements signifies the handiwork of God in the affairs of history. Therefore, we would be wise to see what possible connections these things have with prophecies of the return of the Lord Jesus.

The prophet Daniel was granted an overview of all future history, although some of the visions made him so weak and breathless that an angel had to revive and strengthen him. In the last chapter of Daniel, the prophet admits in his own words that he heard things which he did not understand. "Although I heard, I did not understand. Then I said, "My lord, what shall the end of these things?" And he said, "Go your way, Daniel, for the words are closed up and sealed till the time of the end."[11] What specifically did Daniel not understand? In the first four verses of Daniel 12, the prophet was given a preview of the end times which included a time of great trouble for his people, the Jews. He wanted to know how long it would be before the fulfillment of the things described in the prophecy. The angelic answer was so cryptic that Daniel had to admit that he heard but did not understand, and he asked again. The only explanation given to him was simply that the words were closed up and sealed until the time of the end. This means that only in the time of the end will the explanation become apparent.

If indeed the understanding of the book is sealed until the time of the end, it means that this passage will only be truly understood in the time of the end. The passage immediately before Daniel's question refers to a time of "running to and fro" and to a time when knowledge will be increased. The passage is printed below. You can judge for yourself as to whether they apply to our own time. If you conclude that they do, then you must also conclude that the book is no longer sealed. The unsealing of this passage would mean that it makes sense because it relates to realities of our time, realities which did not exist in previous times. Here is part of what Daniel was told.

> "At that time Michael shall stand up, the great prince who stands watch over the sons of your people; and there shall be a time of trouble, such as never was since there was a nation, even to that time. And at that time your people shall be delivered, every one who is found written in the book. And many of those who sleep in the dust of the earth shall awake, some to everlasting life, some to shame and everlasting contempt. Those who are wise shall shine like the brightness of the firmament, and those who turn many to righteousness like the stars forever and ever. But you, Daniel, shut up the words, and seal the book until the time of the end; many shall run to and fro, and knowledge shall increase."[12]

Visit any international airport today and see how many hundreds of thousands of people are running to and fro across this globe in a single day. Then, look back in history no more than 100 years and recall how people traveled. Overseas travel was limited to slow-moving steamships, and cross-continental travel was limited to steam-powered trains. In so short a time now, jumbo jets carrying 200-300 passengers zoom across the oceans so frequently that their white contrails crisscross the blue sky in ever-changing patterns. Suddenly, horse-drawn carriages have been replaced by high-speed autos and busses; while the rough, muddy highways have become broad ribbons of concrete. Stand for a few moments near a busy eight-lane interstate highway and count, if you can, the number of people "running to and fro!"

Inside many of the thousands of cars which pass you in these few moments, people are on cellular telephones, chatting or conducting business as they drive. Many of the drivers will be listening to Global Positioning Systems, giving them precise, turn-by-turn driving instructions that guide them to their destinations. Still others will be in SUVs or RVs with children in them who are being entertained by television or video game screens mounted in the vehicle's ceiling.

Since television made its debut in the late 1930's, it has rapidly and increasingly become the medium through which the majority of the world population gets its information. In just a few decades, world technology made the quantum jump from radio broadcasting to television broadcasting. When I was a child, my family, like millions of other families across the United States, sat in our home gathered around a radio to hear the evening news. Then, while I was yet a teenager, the pattern changed and families began sitting around a television console, seeing and hearing talking images discuss the world news or acting in some drama or sitcom. Now, with High Definition Broadcasting, space satellite technology and state-of-the-art plasma wide-screen television sets, a vast world population can see international events occurring in real time as clearly as though they were personally present at those events.

For the first time in history, a literal fulfillment of one of Revelation's prophesies is now possible by means of world-wide television. In chapter 11, the Two Witnesses will be killed by the Antichrist in Jerusalem. Then their bodies will lie in the street, and people all over the world will see their bodies lie there for three and a half days. The world celebrates their death, and then will watch in horror as the Two Witnesses rise to their feet and ascend to heaven.

> Then those from the peoples, tribes, tongues, and nations will see their dead bodies three and a half days, and not allow their dead bodies to be put into graves. And those who dwell on the earth will rejoice over them, make merry, and send gifts to one another, because these two prophets tormented those who dwell on the earth. Now after the three and a half days the breath of life from God entered them, and they stood on their feet, and great fear fell on those who saw them.[13]

Please note here the specific use of the words "see" and "saw." This clearly indicates the kind of worldwide, simultaneous, real-time viewing, which although recently impossible, is now possible through the technology of television. Without doubt, we live in the time when this prophecy can be literally fulfilled.

As to the increase of knowledge of which Daniel spoke, look at how we communicate now, in comparison with a century ago. When I was born in 1938, just a single exchange of correspondence by mail usually took two or more weeks. Now, the same exchange can be accomplished in seconds by text-messages with cell phones; or in minutes by email. We once held in ridicule those people who walked around talking to themselves. Now, everywhere you can see adults and children talking with no one else around. Look more closely, and you will see that they have cellular phone devices attached to their ears. Millions of people are in constant conversation with others miles away while driving, or shopping, or at work. Compare with this how information was exchanged even a few decades ago!

With the worldwide web, or Internet, data can be acquired instantly. Not only has information on almost any subject become immediately available, but the amount of that information has increased exponentially. Daniel spoke of a time when knowledge would be increased. The Hebrew word for "increase" is *ravah,* which indicates multiplication rather than addition. The prophecy anticipates an exponential explosion of knowledge. This is the day of the Information Age, and the day of the Information Super-Highway (the Internet). Knowledge is increasing so rapidly that the collective data base doubles in size every 24 months. Of all the scientists who have ever lived, about 80 per cent are alive today. If these things in our time do not indicate the fulfillment of the very conditions described in Daniel's prophecy, it is hard to imagine a world and a time in which there would be better proof of fulfillment. On the other hand, if we are convinced that Daniel's prophecy has become "unsealed" and that these conditions prevail now, we must know that the time of Jesus' return will be very soon now. Are we ready?

There is a spiritual war raging now over the airwaves that are used for all the various forms of broadcasting. Almost since space satellites were first deployed, a race has been going on to gain a monopoly and supremacy in space broadcasting. Christian Broadcasting Network, Trinity Broadcasting Network, and several other Christian enterprises were early adaptors of this technology. Then certain Arab money interests began to throw their financial weight behind development of Moslem-controlled satellite broadcasting. A powerful struggle is now ensuing over the control of broadcasting satellites. According to the Bible, Satan is the prince of the "powers of the air" (Ephesians 2:2). We are told plainly in Ephesians 6:12 that our real war is not against flesh and blood, but that we are dealing with the rulers of darkness and against spiritual forces of evil in the heavenly realms – a reference to Earth's atmosphere.

The news network of Al Jazeera is a Moslem-funded enterprise which uses websites and satellite television to foment global terrorism. It was used repeatedly by terrorist leader Osama Ben Laden to air his video messages to his global following and to make threats against the United States. Twenty-four-hour broadcasting by Al Jazeera promotes the causes of Hezbollah, Hamas, Al Qaeda and other such terrorist groups. The websites are loaded with anti-Israel, anti-U.S., and anti-Christian propaganda. The spiritual war for the minds and hearts of millions has intensified, and it is literally taking place in the atmosphere around the earth, the domain of the prince of the powers of the air. For the first time in history, Satan's territory is being penetrated by Holy Spirit-energized gospel broadcasting. This coincides with a prophesied struggle, in the last days, for control of the "heavens."

That struggle, and the outcome of it, is depicted in Revelation 12:7-12.

> And war broke out in heaven: Michael and his angels fought against the dragon; and the dragon and his angels fought, but they did not prevail; nor was a place for them found in heaven any longer. So the great dragon was cast out, that serpent of old, called

> the Devil and Satan, who deceives the whole world; he was cast to the earth, and his angels were cast out with him. Then I heard a loud voice saying in heaven, "Now salvation, and strength, and the kingdom of our God, and the power of His Christ have come, for the accuser of our brethren, who accused them before our God day and night, has been cast down. And they overcame him by the blood of the Lamb and by the word of their testimony, and they did not love their lives to the death. Therefore rejoice O heavens, and you who dwell in them! Woe to the inhabitants of the earth and the sea! For the devil has come down to you, having great wrath, because he knows that he has a short time."[14]

The battle for the airwaves is only one powerful proof, among many, that Christ is about to return. The big picture, framed by the long perspective of history, is this sudden technological period itself. In the center of that picture we should note man's adventure into space. The past century's incredible increase in knowledge and communication has made possible what we now call the Space Age. Mankind has reached beyond the bounds of earth into space itself. We have stepped on the moon and explored Jupiter, Mars and Saturn. The nations have joined together and built a huge space platform called the Space Lab. In a way, the Space Lab is a repetition of the tower of Babel in modern times. Mankind is once again reaching into the heavens. Once again, God will come down to interrupt the advance of any knowledge-thirsty achievement which refuses to honor Him. This time, God will come down in the Person of the Lord Jesus Christ.

Craze for Pleasure

The Internet has become a modern version of the Tree of Knowledge of Good and Evil which was the object of temptation in the Garden of Eden. The Internet provides instant gratification to all who seek knowledge, whether good or evil. Today's "forbidden fruit" is pornography. Pornography dominates the Internet to the extent that almost any child with a computer can find pornographic photo galleries and videos; and can study all forms of sexual perversions for hours at a time. Let me say here that the Internet can be also used for pursuit of the knowledge of truth. Many churches and ministries today have websites which offer free biblical studies. Many Christian colleges and universities offer training for ministry through online courses. Sadly, however, the Information Superhighway allows huge populations of children and youth all over the world to have unbridled access to every form of evil.

The craze for sexual pleasure extends far beyond the use of the Internet for pornography. In our time, the number two criminal industry in the world (second only to illegal drug trafficking) is the child sex slave industry. Children in many Asian countries are routinely sold by their parents into slavery. Even in the cities of America, children are kidnapped and disappear into the underground sex industry. In one of the most recent high school fads, naïve teenage girls have used the built-in cameras on cell phones to post nude pictures of themselves on the Internet, where predators may find them. These photos find their way into porn web sites as well. There are also married women who, because of boredom or a desire for quick profit, willingly enter in the underground porn industry.

The Bible prophecies a time in the last days when people will love pleasure more than they love God, and throw off all restraints as they follow their sensual passions. In the following passage from 2 Timothy, note that the lovers of evil pleasure are the sort who creep into households and make captives of gullible women who are led away by all kinds of lusts. They are always experimenting and learning new things, but never coming to the knowledge of truth. In other words, they, like Eve in the Garden, can only derive evil knowledge from what they are doing. "Creeping into households" can now be done by way of the Internet. The following words from Second Timothy 3 were written around A.D. 67, but they describe our time.

> But know this, that in the last days perilous times will come: for men will be lovers of themselves, lovers of money, boasters, proud, blasphemers, disobedient to parents, unthankful, unholy, unloving, unforgiving, slanderers, without self-control, brutal, despisers of good, traitors, headstrong, haughty, lovers of pleasure rather than lovers of God, having a form of godliness but denying its power. And from such people turn away! For of this sort are those who creep into households and make captives of gullible women loaded down with sins, led away by various lusts, always learning and never able to come to the knowledge of the truth.[15]

We live today in an age which is easily described by the passage above. Go to any modern shopping mall and note how many shops, arcades and stores capitalize on the craze for pleasure. Observe the number of video stores, game machine arcades, risqué lingerie stores and theaters. Listen to the background music and look at the posters in the teen clothing stores. On any busy street, note how much of today's clothing fashion has evolved to accent and maximize sensuality. Visit any major auto dealership and see how selfish pleasure is used as a marketing tool for this year's "hottest and sexiest" car models. Watch television and see the overwhelming propensity to push programming beyond all moral limits. Surely, this craze for sensual pleasure is one of the signs that we are in the last days before the return of Christ.

European Union

The dream of a united Europe has existed for centuries. Charlemagne and Napoleon failed in their attempts to rule all of Europe. In the last century, Kaiser Wilhelm II and Adolf Hitler of Germany pursued the same dream and failed. In a 1989 interview, Mikhail Gorbachev spoke of a united Europe "from the Atlantic to the Ural Mountains." Thirty years earlier, Charles de Gaulle expressed the same idea in almost the same words.[16] Yet, with so many nations involved, all with diverse language, religious, ethnic and governmental structures, continental unity has remained an elusive dream. Nevertheless, where political and military attempts at European unity have ultimately fallen apart, the motivation of economic survival is apparently succeeding. The European Community, first formed in 1958, has become the European Union of today. Today, its 27 member nations and 500 million citizens comprise a powerful economic community which accounts for 30% of the world's GNP: equivalent to $16.8 trillion U.S. dollars.

Is this the beginning of a mighty political and military entity which could be ruled by a single government? In other words, could this become the platform for the reign of the Antichrist of biblical prophecy? Is this the beginning of a European government that will even control Israel in the last days? No one knows (except God) if the present situation in Europe will produce a government which will also rule Israel. But the Bible does show that ancient Rome will rise again, and that it will again control the nation of Israel in the last days. The same Gentile power which ruled Israel at the time of Jesus' first coming will be ruling Israel at the time of His second coming. The Jews today have returned to their ancient homeland, never to be removed again. That is the clear teaching of Scripture which we have already reviewed. Although the nation will never again be destroyed, it is probable that Israel will suffer domination from Rome once again in the very last years of this age. There are some compelling biblical reasons for believing this.

According to most conservative scholars, Daniel prophesied a last-days revival of the Roman Empire. This renewed nation will be the one which is to be crushed by the arrival of Messiah and His kingdom. The coming of the first Roman Empire was predicted in Daniel 2 and 7; yet that empire did not end with the first coming of Jesus, so we may be sure that the first coming of Jesus was not the establishment of an everlasting kingdom to which Daniel referred. Furthermore, the first Roman Empire was not ended with a second coming of Jesus. There must be yet a future time in which Messiah will come to destroy the Roman Empire and establish His millennial reign on Earth. That is when "the kingdom and dominion, and the greatness of the kingdoms under the whole heaven, shall be given to the people, the saints of the Most High. His kingdom is an everlasting kingdom, and all dominions shall serve and obey Him."[17] The Messianic kingdom has not yet come, and Europe has not yet developed into another Roman empire.

In Daniel 9, the prophet gives an amazing timetable summary of events relating to Israel, starting with the rebuilding of Jerusalem after the Babylonian Captivity. There would be 483 years of history ending with the killing of the Messiah. Then there would be a gap in the timetable, before the final seven years of prophetic history. In this gap would come the destruction of the rebuilt Jerusalem (at the time of Daniel's prophecy, it was still laid waste from the Babylonian destruction). We know from history that Jerusalem was rebuilt shortly after the time of Daniel, and then was destroyed by the Romans in A.D. 70. In Daniel's timetable gap, there would be an unspecified period of multiple "desolations" of the city (which brings us to modern times). Then the timetable would resume; precisely when a future Roman ruler confirms a covenant with Israel.

The identity of this ruler is not clearly stated in Daniel's prophecy. The leader who establishes the covenant, or treaty, with Israel is simply called "he" in Daniel 9:27. The closest antecedent to "he" is found in verse 26, where the prophet speaks of "the people of the ruler who is to come" (the people who destroyed Jerusalem and the temple). Since this was done by an army of the Roman Empire, it is reasonable to think that the ruler, who will at first protect and later persecute Israel, will be a ruler of a future empire of Rome. In the book of Revelation, John affirms the ancient prophecy of Daniel and again pictures a leader rising from a ten-nation confederacy. Both Daniel and John describe an awful period of persecution in Israel for three and one-half years. John wrote Revelation around A.D. 96. In John's prophecy, this three and one-half years of persecution by the Antichrist was still future.

One of the signs that we may be living in the last days is the unification of Europe, in much of what was once the territory of ancient Rome. Germany has reunited. Other reunifications may follow, resulting in a reduction in the number of member nations in the European Union to exactly ten. We may soon see the establishment of Rome as the permanent capital of the European Union. The central government will gain additional power to control its member states, much as the United States government consolidated its federal power over once largely independent states. Currently, 21 member nations of the European Union are also members of NATO. The architects of the European Union intend that, eventually, all individual nations of the European Union will relinquish control of their armies to a central command. Then we will see one commander-in-chief, a ruler who has the power to command an army more powerful than that of the United States. This new Roman ruler will be in charge of exactly the kind of revived Empire foretold by Daniel. He is the probable one who will broker a Middle East peace treaty (the covenant with "many"). That is the signal that the prophetic clock in Daniel's timetable has started ticking again! When that happens, the world will surely be approaching the end.

Worldwide Revival of Christianity

Prophecy scholars point to a world-wide evangelistic harvest at the end of the age. This prediction is based upon passages such as Romans 11:12-30, which speaks of a mass conversion by Israel. This passage ties a worldwide acceptance of God's grace to the time of Israel's conversion. Another passage related to this subject is found in Revelation 7:4-9, which relates a vision of 144,000 divinely-sealed Jewish evangelists who will witness in the last days. Verse 9 shows the result of their labor. "After these things I looked, and behold, a great multitude which no one could number, of all nations, tribes, peoples, and tongues, standing before the throne and before the Lamb, clothed with white robes, with palm branches in their hands."[18] Such an uncountable multitude of new believers could only result from the activity of robustly healthy Christianity; definitely not a defeated and declining world movement. Therefore, the greatest worldwide revival of Christianity is yet to happen.

The religion of Islam is spreading rapidly across the world today, by birth rate, conversions and by governmental decree. *Sharia* law, which favors the growth of Islam is being systematically instituted, even in non-Moslem countries. Surprisingly, however, the fastest growing religious movement in the world today is not Islam. The Pentecostal form of Christianity is spreading at a far greater rate than Christianity as a whole. According to a recent article by CBN News senior reporter Dale Hurd,[19] there are already more Pentecostals worldwide than Buddhists. Today there are more than 80 million Christians in the Peoples Republic of China, and they have a burden to take the Gospel to Moslems across the globe.

Evangelistic growth is but one precursor to revival. Another is a commitment to intense prayer. Several key developments at the dawn of the new millennium indicate the greatest commitment to prayer in Christian history. On June 25, 1994, twelve million Christians in 179 countries participated in the March for Jesus, and in that year a record 160 million Christians were committed to daily prayer for world revival.[20] There are now approximately 1,300 global prayer networks, including ten million prayer groups, committed to daily prayer for evangelism and revival. A third precursor to revival which can be mentioned here is cooperation among the many evangelistic denominations. More than 300 global world missions agencies now work in cooperation under three major umbrella organizations. Never before has there been such an organized effort to strategically deploy missionary personnel, ships, aircraft, broadcasting and print media to take the Gospel to every nation in our time.

When all of these things are considered, one must conclude that we are truly on the verge of the prophetic last great revival of Christianity. Perhaps the revival itself will only occur worldwide in the perilous time immediately preceding the Great Tribulation. Jesus spoke of this period before the Great Tribulation as the "beginning of sorrows" (birth pangs). The birth pangs may signal the birth of many new souls in the Kingdom! Perhaps history's greatest Christian community will not form until faced with the hardships of a world falling apart and the challenges of worldwide persecution. But when this tumultuous time begins and never-before-heard-of numbers turn to Christ, we can note yet another convincing sign of the Lord's near return.

World Religion Based Upon Astrology

Astrology will be a central motif in a united world religion just before end of this age. Astrology is a pseudo science, not to be confused with the true science of astronomy. Astrology makes predictions and interprets life according to the supposed positions and movements of the moon, planets and star constellations in a calendar year. The story of astrology as a religious movement began with the Tower of Babel in Genesis 11. It was then that they said, "Come let us build ourselves a city with a tower that reaches to the heavens…"[21] The Tower of Babel was a prototype of the ziggurat towers, whose ruins dot the landscape of Iraq today. In almost every case, there is evidence of idolatrous worship of the sun, moon, planets and stars. Babylon is a code name for a great system of false religion which is intended to replace the worship of God. As Bible scholar and teacher John F. Walvoord has explained, "Babylon is actually a counterfeit or pseudo religion which plagued Israel in the Old Testament as well as the church in the New Testament, and which, subsequent to apostolic days, has had a tremendous influence in moving the church from biblical simplicity to apostate confusion."[22]

In the time of the divided kingdoms, the northern kingdom of Israel was destroyed, in part, by the astrological religion which began at Babel. "And they left all the commandments of the LORD their God, and made them molten images, even two calves, and made a grove, and worshiped all the host of heaven, and served Baal."[23] The worship of the "host of heaven" was included in this summary statement of all of Israel's pagan practices which led to Israel's fall in 722 B.C. The practice of worshiping the stars, imported from Mesopotamia, continued in the days of Isaiah and Jeremiah. Each prophet in his turn preached against this insidious pagan religion, which would eventually bring down the judgment of God upon Judah as well.

In Isaiah's time, the wicked king Manasseh in Judah promoted the same idolatrous worship. King Manasseh promoted the worship of the "host of heaven," a reference to the sun, moon, planets and stars. "And he built altars for all the host of heaven in the two courts of the house of the LORD."[24] Perhaps Manasseh, in his wickedness, thought it would be wise to adopt the religion of Babylon, Judah's greatest military threat. Isaiah predicted that Babylon would destroy Judah as an instrument of God's judgment; but that Babylon would also receive the judgment of God. Babylon, which was ruled by this astrological religion, was singled out in Isaiah's preaching. "All the counsel you have received has only worn you out! Let your astrologers come forward, those stargazers who make predictions month by month, let them save you from what is coming upon you."[25] Jeremiah, long after the time of Isaiah, also condemned the astrological rituals practiced in Judah. These rites may have been encouraged in the atmosphere of appeasement and syncretism as the influence of Babylon increasingly dominated the region, but Jeremiah severely condemned it. "The houses in Jerusalem and those of the kings of Judah will be defiled like this place, Topheth – all the houses where they burned incense on the roofs to all the starry hosts and poured out drink offerings to other gods."[26]

This background gives us the keys needed to unlock the meaning of an enigmatic statement in Revelation 17:5. In the symbolic language so characteristic of apocalyptic literature, the writer John describes the "Great Harlot" of the Tribulation Period. "And on her forehead a name was written: MYSTERY, BABYLON THE GREAT, THE MOTHER OF HARLOTS AND OF THE ABOMINATIONS OF THE EARTH."[27] Any good hermeneutical approach to the book of Revelation requires knowledge of the rest of the Bible, from which the symbols are drawn.

This system will be worldwide and will be in place in the last days just before the return of Christ. It will encourage persecution of true Christianity and enjoy the martyrdom of believers in the last days. Note these words from Revelation 17:6: "and I saw the woman drunk with the blood of the saints, and with the blood of the martyrs of Jesus."[28] "The history of the Church has demonstrated that apostate Christendom is unsparing in its persecution of those who attempt to maintain a true faith in Jesus Christ. What has been true in the past will be brought to its ultimate intensity in this future time, when martyrs will be beyond number from every kindred, tongue and nation."[29]

Let's get back to astrology. What has astrology to do with the future worldwide religious system? Throughout biblical history, astrology was associated with the false systems. The code name of Babylon is drawn from the real name "Babel" which later gave it name to the Babylonian Empire. From the beginning, the name has always been associated with a false religion that involves astrology. Even outside of biblical history, one can observe this one common feature in the religious practices of all ancient pagan cultures. One of the most bloodthirsty of all ancient cultures was that of the Maya in Central America. I have visited many ruins there and have personally seen the altars where human beings were sacrificed. Today, among the archaeological excavations, many of their religious observatories are found intact; and professional guides at these sites will demonstrate to visitors how the Maya tracked the movements of the heavenly bodies.

"What's your sign?" It's not an unusual question in current society. Today, one of the most popular worldwide movements is astrology. In newspapers, a favorite feature for many is the section on the daily horoscope. Some people cannot start their day without it. Fortune tellers depend heavily upon astrological signs. On the Internet, misguided lonely people seek friends and lovers who were born under the same "sign." When party-goers are introduced to one another, one of the first things mentioned is the "sign" one was born under. Witches and Satanists use astrological signs in the practice of their cults. "New-agers" refer to astrological signs in their belief systems. Soon, a world network of religions will also embrace astrology while it promotes evil and persecutes Christianity. The world climate for this development exists today. It cannot be long before the false system takes it final form and incorporates astrology as a common feature.

Environmental Crisis

Is "global warming" real, or not? That has been one of the major controversies since the dawn of the new millennium. Part of the contention about global warming is the issue of whether or not it is a part of a natural cycle which has occurred throughout earth's history. There are many other environmental issues which have become significant concerns to scientists and to world leaders. Entire crop years in agricultural regions are being lost due to unusual disruptions in weather patterns: droughts, floods and storms. New, more intense solar storms are predicted, which will drastically affect weather (as well as cell phones and GPS devices). One of the biblical prophesies of the last days concerns the heat of the sun. "Then the fourth angel poured out his bowl upon the sun, and power was given to him to scorch men with fire, and men were scorched with great heat..."[30]

Fishermen are complaining that their industries are being destroyed because of pollution in rivers and seas. In the book of Revelation, the pollution of rivers is one of the seven last trumpet judgments which will occur at the opening of the seventh and last seal. "Then the third angel sounded: and a great star fell from heaven, burning like a torch, and it fell on a third of the rivers and on the springs of water; and the name of the star is Wormwood; and a third of the waters became wormwood; and many men died from the water, because it was made bitter."[31] It is interesting to note that the Russian word *Chernobyl* means "wormwood." Pollution of air and water by nuclear radiation is now a greater potentially, because of the existence of terrorist groups attempting to use small, hand-carried nuclear devices as "dirty bombs" which would create "dead zones" of radiation.

Bird and bee populations are declining. According to the Birdlife International World Conference in 2008, "Birds are in decline across the world, providing evidence of a rapid deterioration in the global environment that is affecting all life on earth."[32] Moreover, honeybees are dying in large numbers. In the U.S., 800,000 hives were wiped out in 2007 and a further million died in 2008.[33] Albert Einstein once said, "If the bee disappeared off the surface of the globe, then man would only have four years of life left. No more pollination, no more plants, no more animals, no more man."[34] Whether this statement is true or not, there are abundant indications that the world is headed toward an environmental crisis. Political leaders will use environmental issues to gain power, but it is illogical to rely upon governments to reverse global trends. It is apparent to students of the Bible that the planet is groaning under the weight of the curse of sin, and it is a reminder that the world cannot continue forever as it is. How much longer before Jesus comes?

One World Movement

Prophecy seems to strongly indicate a one-world government near the end of time. The fulfillment of some specific predictions would logically require a single all-powerful global government. One such prediction is a worldwide numbering system for regulation of all buying and selling, foretold in Revelation 13:16-18. Another is the worldwide coalition of armies which will oppose Christ at His coming, mentioned in Psalm 2, Zechariah 12 and Revelation 19. The

Bible foretells of a world leader in Revelation 6:2 and 13:7, who will have authority "over every tribe, tongue, and nation."[35] Obviously, if there is to be a one-world government led by a single dictator, the formation of such a global government would require a process over time. In the season of time just prior to the second coming of Christ, we should anticipate various one-world movements. First, regional groups of nations will unite for economic and military purposes. But organizations of nations which will surrender their own sovereignty to a central government and a central legal system will come later. These will arise out of a series of man-made or natural disasters.

"Get US out of the UN!" So read crude highway signs in the 1960's, 1970's and 1980's during the "heat" of the "Cold" War. It was feared that the United Nations was the beginning of a one-world government; and that the US would soon lose its sovereignty. Actually, the present United Nations cannot even manage its own building in New York. That building is in disrepair and even janitorial service is poor. The UN passes resolutions but really has no power to enforce them. The troops which it deploys for peacekeeping purposes are joint operations by participating countries. Wherever they are deployed, they usually wind up in observer roles. It is no longer likely that the United Nations will develop into a global government.

There are several global institutions (such as the International Criminal Court, International Monetary Fund and United Nations) and other international organizations (such as African Union, Association of Southeast Asian Nations, European Union, Organization of American States and Union of South American Nations) which may be considered as the seeds of a world government system. The best-known model for the step-by-step establishment of a global government is the European Union (EU), which has already been discussed. It gives some degree of governmental unity for over 500 million people in 27 countries, providing open borders, a parliament, a court system, common currency and a joint market economy; and it is still evolving.

Perhaps surprisingly, however, even larger global models than the European Union are emerging. The African Union (AU), established in 2002, currently has 53 African countries in its membership. The African Union aims to form a single defense force, have only one currency, have a cabinet, and a head of state. The Shanghai Cooperation Organization (SCO) was established in 2001 by the People's Republic of China, Russia, Kazakhstan, Kyrgyzstan, Tajikistan and Uzbekistan. Its area of influence is much larger than the European Union and African Union combined. There is also the South Asian Association for Regional Cooperation (SAARC) which was established in 1985 and currently has eight member nations with a total population of 1.5 billion.[36]

There is currently no such thing as a one-world government, or anything which comes close. An organization made up of delegates from various nations known as Parliamentarians for Global Action have promoted the idea of global government; but as of yet, it has received little international attention.[37] There is no functioning global government which has jurisdiction over the whole world. The member nations are so divided, because of geographical, demographical, religious and political differences, that governmental unity is practically impossible. However, it is conceivable that some international catastrophe or crisis might cause the more powerful nations to forget their differences and unite in a one-world government. This might not be through the United Nations. It could more easily be through the European Union or the Shanghai

Cooperation Organization, whose member nations are accustomed to totalitarian government. When the major nuclear powers combine under one government, the less powerful nations would of course soon be forced to cooperate. That would produce such scenarios as we see in prophesies of the last days. The movement toward regional unification of nations, as demonstrated in the examples mentioned above, has especially escalated in the past decade. This may mean that we are fast approaching the time of the end.

In this chapter, we have briefly identified and described some of the world conditions which, according to our understanding of the Bible, are to be considered as signs of the second coming of the Lord Jesus. We have purposely avoided giving much space to the Antichrist and to his reign of terror during the Tribulation period. To do so would require a much larger volume than this; and yet mainly consist of what can be found in hundreds of other prophecy books. As in the previous chapters, our focus remains on the signs of the coming of Jesus. It is hoped that readers will be convinced that prophesies are being fulfilled, and that there are sound reasons to believe that we are in the season of His coming. We are not describing timetables, but the times themselves.

ENDNOTES FOR CHAPTER SEVEN

1. Second Thessalonians 1:3-4
2. Second Timothy 3:1-5
3. Jude 17-19
4. Second Peter 3:3-4
5. Second Thessalonians 2:11-12
6. Revelation 18:4
7. Revelation 9:20-21
8. Isaiah 19b-20
9. Revelation 12:15
10. Revelation 12:11
11. Daniel 12:8-9
12. Daniel 12:1-4
13. Revelation 11:9-11
14. Revelation 12:7-12
15. Second Timothy 3:1-7
16. Charles H. Dyer, World News and Bible Prophecy. (Wheaton, IL: Tyndale House, 1993), 185
17. Daniel 7:27
18. Revelation 7:9
19. http://www.cbn.com/CBNNews/News/030819a.aspx, December 22, 2008
20. Andres Tapia, "Is World Ripe For Revival?" Christianity Today November 14, 1994; December 22, 2008
21. Genesis 11:4a NIV
22. John F. Walvoord, The Revelation of Jesus Christ. (Chicago: Moody Press, 1966), 246
23. Second Kings 17:16 KJV
24. Second Kings 21:5
25. Isaiah 47:13 NIV
26. Jeremiah 19:13 NIV
27. Revelation 17:5
28. Revelation 17:6
29. Walvoord, ibid, 247
30. Revelation 16:8-9a
31. Revelation 8:10-11
32. http://www.rspb.org.uk/news/details.asp?id=tcm:9-199218, 12/24/2008
33. http://www.guardian.co.uk/books/2008/jul/20/scienceandnature, 12/24/2008
34. Ibid.
35. Revelation 13:7c
36. http://en.wikipedia.org/wiki/World_government, 12/27/2008
37. Ibid.

Chapter Eight

HEAVEN AT LAST

A LARGE AIRPORT is an impressive and exciting place – at least, for a country boy like me. The concourses are jammed with thousands of people who are going places! Crowds of people stepping quickly toward gates with tickets in hand and bags in tow! But not everyone at an airport is having an exciting day. One day, my attention fell on such a person. He worked at the airport every day. For him, it was another busy day on the job. Behind the counter at the airport newsstand, he scarcely looked up at customers as he rang up their purchases. He limited his conversational interchange to only a few words per person: "Will that be all today? ...That's ten dollars and sixty cents. ...Out of eleven? ...Your change is forty cents. ...Have a good day." He repeated the same conversation over and over for hours every day. Announcements of flight departures to exotic and far-off destinations poured through the airport public address system, but he did not hear them. Why should he? He was not planning to go anywhere that day. The flight announcements were only background noise in his daily workday world. I think that's how it is with a lot of nominal Christians. These prophecies of the Second Coming are like the airport flight announcements were for that airport worker: just background noise! The signs of His coming are of little interest to those who don't have their minds on Heaven.

We cannot study the Second Coming without also dealing with Heaven. The signs of His coming are relevant in our personal lives only to the extent that we are thinking about Heaven. If Heaven is not real to us, then there is not much point in discussing the event when Jesus will come to take us there. Perhaps you have been preoccupied with your own weekly and daily routine, and you really aren't giving much thought, if any, to what Heaven will be like. Sure, you've already decided you'd rather go to Heaven than to Hell. And you've received Christ as Lord. But so far, you just can't get your mind on Heaven. When conversations occasionally touch upon Heaven, you find it a bit awkward. There could be some good reasons for that. I've written this chapter just for you.

The Main Message of the Bible

Imagine being put on the spot by an open-minded non-Christian. "Okay, so you say the Holy Bible is the Word of God to *all* mankind. What does it say to *me*? Can you sum it up in ten minutes or less?" How would you answer? Most Christians – many of whom are seminary-trained, cannot provide a satisfying answer, even when allowed much more time than ten minutes to do so. We all can point to a great many things that the Bible says, but not many of us can put its main message into only a few words. Yet, as many of my former students will tell you, "a thing clearly perceived can be briefly told."

Think about it. If the same Bible that carried God's message centuries ago is still God's message today, then its main message has to be a simple, timeless, unchangeable truth. That message has to be easy to grasp. It should have been easily understandable to those in previous centuries who did not have the light of modern scholarship. It should be easily understandable today to us who did not have the advantage of being the first hearers; and therefore do not have the cultural context with which to interpret the message. And it should be easily understood by all educational levels and cultural backgrounds. We should be able to communicate it today simply and succinctly. What is the *main message of the Bible*?

Here it is. The Bible is a book about Heaven and how to get there. The main message of the Bible is that God has planned for you to have a redeemed life in a redeemed body on a redeemed Earth. Even the Heaven where God is now is not God's final destination for you. He intends to remake the planet Earth in perfection and dwell on it with you. Our home in eternity will actually be a completed and perfected Earth where everything works right and nothing wears out and nobody dies. Everything is beautiful and everybody lives in peace and joy. God is making this available to you through a living relationship with the risen Lord Jesus Christ. There is a default destination for those who reject God's plan in favor of their own. It's a very real place called Hell. But God's offer to you is a place in the Kingdom of Heaven. *That* is the main message of the Bible.

Are you surprised? Probably! We live in a time when the church does not say much about Heaven. Yet, up until only the last few decades, the doctrine of Heaven was historically held in great importance by the Church. It was a central theme and a life-sustaining conviction. Not only has the modern church shown little interest in Heaven, but the sketchy notions that come to mind when Heaven is mentioned are grossly distorted. Almost every poll shows that an overwhelming majority of Americans continue to believe that there is life after death and that heaven and hell exist. But what they actually believe about Heaven varies widely. To borrow a term from Internet usage, people are "cutting and pasting" ideas from a mixture of sources that include television, movies, conversations with friends, and books about near-death experiences.

Only a fraction of what the Bible itself says about Heaven is ever taught in Bible colleges or seminaries. It is normally dealt with in just one lesson in a Systematic Theology course; and that usually as only one part of the general subject, "The Eternal State." Therefore, there is little wonder that most modern pastors neglect the subject. Moreover, because their pastors say little about Heaven, congregations are likely to falsely assume that the Bible doesn't have much to say about Heaven. Rarely emphasized except at funerals, and then only described as something like an unending church service, Heaven has been presented as a mysterious and somewhat boring afterlife. We are taught that it's good to go to Heaven, because it's better than Hell; but we know very little about Heaven itself!

Try to picture this imaginary scenario: two astronauts have trained for seven years for just one specific purpose. They are about to make the first manned space flight to Mars. As they sit atop the huge rocket during countdown, one asks the other, "Do you know anything about what it will be like on Mars?" To which the other replies, "Next to nothing. It didn't come up in any of the training sessions. I guess we'll find out everything when we get there." There's a similar attitude held by many people about Heaven. "We'll understand it better by and by," as the song goes. Strangely the same people mull over maps and make meticulous preparations to travel to another country. They want to know as much as possible about the other country.

What will Heaven be like? Will it be, as some portray, an unending church service? Will we still be the persons we are now? Will we look so different we won't recognize each other? What will our bodies be like? What will it be like to finally see God the Father and Jesus? What will the angels look like? What will we do? Will we come back to earth? These and many other questions crowd into our minds when we think about Heaven. Jesus says in Revelation 21, verse 5: "Behold, I make all things new." What can be known about the "new" things of Heaven? Happily, the Bible does not hide this information from us. It is there for us to read and treasure in our hearts.

We can focus upon seven great realities of Heaven. First, we will be face to face with our Savior, Jesus Christ. We will see Him in all of His rightful glory as the Prince of Heaven, at the right hand of God our Father. Second, we will see only redeemed mankind about us – everyone that is righteous and holy. We will reign together with Christ over all the far reaches of the entire universe. Third, we will be based on a redeemed earth, pure and pristine, with the Shekinah glory of God lighting the entire planet. There will be no night there. Fourth, we will dwell in the Heavenly Jerusalem, God's home, which has been moved to Earth. It will be the seat of government and a place of continual worship. Fifth, we will have perfect resurrection bodies. They will be as physical as the body of Jesus which He took to Heaven, or the bodies of Enoch and Elijah who went to Heaven without physical death. Heaven is a real place for real people! Yet, these bodies will be glorified with a magnified spirit-nature and fully-developed minds. Sixth, we will be part of God's great Church, described in Hebrews 12:22-23. The Church, as an assembly of the called-out ones, will exist for God's glory throughout all eternity, according to Ephesians 3:21. It will be the community of love which God has always planned. Seventh, we will see the fulfillment of all our greatest and highest visions and dreams. Works for which God has fashioned us, though cut short by death or physical handicaps here, will reach their completion there.

The words of Paul Bilheimer are appropriate here. "God's purpose in the plan of redemption – to produce, by means of the new birth, an entirely new and unique species, exact replicas of His Son, with whom He will share His glory and His dominion, and who will constitute a royal progeny and for the governing and administrative staff of His eternal kingdom."[1] God wants us to be conformed to the image of His Son. He has made us joint heirs with Christ. We can become more Christlike in this life, but only in the enhanced capacities of our glorified bodies can we be fully conformed to the image of Jesus. That is what we were designed for; and why our souls are restlessly longing for eternity.

What is our divinely designed destiny? Our Father went to great length to give us opportunity not to die as sinners and face an eternal Hell, but to receive a new birth that makes us heirs of the Kingdom! How we ought to thank and praise God for His great love that embraced us before the foundation of the world and planned for our salvation through the gift of His unique Son. Jesus' death on the cross for our sins signifies the enormity of our sin. Such a desperate measure would never have been taken if there were any other way to be saved! But His death also signifies the enormity of His love for us! Moreover, it demonstrates the purity and power of the sinless blood of our Saviour which was shed for us on the cross. What power there is in the blood of Jesus! The power that loved and redeemed us is also the power for productive enterprises as God's people in eternity.

Although in God's Word there are many theological themes, all of which ought to be carefully studied, it is clear that the main message of the Bible is the offer of Heaven to lost mankind. Satan has almost succeeded in making Heaven so mysterious and unappealing that many have no interest. Yet the word of God tells us to focus on Heaven. We are to set our minds on heavenly things. We are to lay up treasure in Heaven. We are to live not for this world, but the world to come. Our Lord Jesus who came from Heaven and returned to Heaven promises us that He will come for us and receive us to Himself, so that we can dwell with Him and Father God in Heaven. But more than that, He will reclaim Earth itself and make it into a heavenly paradise similar to the Garden of Eden. No one in his right mind can possibly conceive of an afterlife of boredom when he understands what Heaven will actually be.

There is much available knowledge about Heaven. I challenge the reader to search the scriptures for mentions of a "new heaven" or "new earth." Read the prophecies of Isaiah about what life will be like when God creates new heavens and a new earth. Read again the teachings of Jesus on the "Kingdom of Heaven" (Matthew's unique term) or the "Kingdom of God." Check out some good theological books that deal with Heaven. Find and consider descriptions of Heaven in the writings of such great students of God's Word as Anthony Hoekema, C. S. Lewis, A. H. Hodge, Ray C. Stedman, A. W. Tozer, Sidlow Baxter, John Piper, David Chilton and Richard Mouw. Conduct your own studies about Heaven. The information which is available is more than enough to start you talking with everybody about Heaven! But while you study, please make sure of two things. First, make certain that you are on your way to Heaven.

Second, make sure you know everything that God's Word says about the place that will be your home for all eternity.

I pray that your inquiry into the subject of Heaven will open a whole new horizon of hope for you. When Columbus discovered the Western Hemisphere, Spain had coins minted with the Latin motto, *Plus Ultra*. The phrase means "More Beyond."[2] What a mind-expanding expression that must have been – for people who thought that the world which they knew was all that existed! The biblical message is that beyond this life there is more. Much more! Can you imagine the glories of the new heavens! Why has God surrounded us with such an amazing creation, filled with marvels that we can only partially see through telescopes and microscopes? I think it is to stir our imaginations. We should never be bored with our life in Christ. There is so much more beyond – *Plus Ultra!* Think of all the spiral, pinwheel and elliptical shaped galaxies, in their brilliant effusion of colors, sparkling throughout the vast expanses of space. They say this universe is past its peak – winding down. Yet God has promised to make it all new, just as He will make us all new! As Randy Alcorn put it, "If we know Jesus, you and I, we who will never pass our peaks will be there to behold an endless revelation of natural wonders that display God's glory…with nothing to block our view."[3]

I have attempted in the foregoing paragraphs to help you start thinking more concretely about Heaven. If we properly understand what God has in store for us, every sign of the Second Coming will be of immense interest to us. The signs are meant to alert us and raise our attention from earthly to heavenly things. With our minds on Heaven, we cannot help but hope that Jesus will come soon. The Rapture is not so much about a time of leaving here as it is about a time of arriving there. Hebrews 11:5, in mentioning the translation of Enoch, uses the Greek word *metatithemi.* It means "to transfer to another place." In the Rapture, Jesus will transfer us to a place. Heaven is a real place.

When You See Jesus

The first Person in your field of sight after the moment of the Rapture will most certainly be your Lord and Saviour, King Jesus. You will see Him face to face in all His true glory. When you see Jesus, sensations within you will abound and will be magnified beyond your wildest imagination. There will be sight, sound and feeling. First, there is sight. Jesus will appear to you in a shining body as He did in the Transfiguration, and as He appeared to John on the island of Patmos. His appearance will be so awesomely appealing that you can see nothing and no one else except Him. Then there will be sound. I expect to hear the sound of the most wonderfully tender and assuring voice saying, "Well done. Welcome to your Father's house!" Then there will surely be feeling: the softest, warmest and most comforting embrace you have ever longed for. When you see Jesus, your heart will experience the inner fullness for which it was made, and for which it has always sought. You will be overwhelmed with satisfaction! For the first time in a literal sense, your life will be complete.

What color is Jesus? As I have traveled for years through vastly varied cultures, I have noted that the artists of the world have very different ideas on the skin color of Jesus. Asians paint Him yellow; Native Americans paint Him red; Africans paint Him black. Latin Americans paint Him tan and Europeans paint Him white. It was amazingly appropriate for the Savior of all nations to enter the human stream in a Semitic body, with a pigmentation approximating the composite of all the skin colors of the world! When we see Him again, he will be neither white nor black; tan nor red, nor yellow. He will appear as He did in the Transfiguration: a shining form that radiates pure white light, which is itself a mixture of all colors.

The Throne Room, which is the tangible, manifest expression of God the Father's presence, is the central focus of Heaven. Jesus will take you into the Father's presence, where you will see our Creator-Father in all His holiness and majesty. The Bible describes God's throne. John was permitted to see it, and describes it in the fourth chapter of Revelation. Surrounded by the flaming seraphim and the hovering cherubim, God's throne has the appearance of crystal, and sits on a crystal platform. The throne is surrounded by a glowing aura, as green as emerald. The figure of God is like a glowing diamond with flashes of fire emanating from Him, and his crystal throne flashes with lightning. There are seven lamps of Spirit-fire burning before the throne, and from the throne come awesome thunderings and voices. The throne room is the ultimate atmosphere for worship. All the elders and saints are bowing before Him and adoring Him. Your worship of the Father in that place will come to you as naturally as an adoring child responds to a loving father.

To Actually See God

A persistent yearning deep within all of us, no matter how long suppressed, is the desire to actually see God. Over the years, several friends and acquaintances have had near-death, out-of-body experiences. They all described a moment, just before they were brought back, when they were about to see God. In each case, they were initially overwhelmed by a sense of disappointment when they regained consciousness. One of my friends, Howard Conatser, had two such encounters. After the second, he authored a small book titled, "I've Got to Find My Father." Of all the things we may think we want, this is the one thing for which we were created: to see God and to please Him. He is what our soul longs for. As David said in Psalm 27:4, "One thing have I desired of the Lord, that will I seek: That I may dwell in the house of the Lord all the days of my life, to behold the beauty of the Lord, and to inquire in His temple." *God is the central idea of Heaven.* Being in Heaven means being with God – at last! God's finest and most magnificent gift He will ever give us is Himself! When we see the Father, we will finally comprehend completely that Jesus is, as the writer of Hebrews told us, the express image of the Father![4]

We are told in Revelation 22:4 that God's servants will "see His face." That has been a privilege withheld from fallen humanity. In the Old Testament, God told Moses that he could not see His face, for no one could do that and live. God is so awesomely majestic and holy, and we are so small and unholy, that the idea of seeing God's face is really incredible. The New Testament elsewhere tells us that God lives "in unapproachable light, whom no one has seen or can see."[5] That is why we are told in Hebrews to follow "holiness, without which no one will see the Lord."[6] We can only obtain acceptable holiness through Jesus. He, as our Great High Priest, has offered His own blood so that we may come with confidence into the Most Holy Place.[7] Through our relationship with the Son, according to God's Word, we can now "come boldly to the throne of grace…"[8] We have the promise of Jesus, Himself. He taught us, "Blessed are the pure in heart, for they will see God."[9] *What will it be like to see the Maker of the entire Universe?*

How can we "see" God, when God is a Spirit-Being? Jesus said in John 4:24 that God is spirit. References to human-like parts of the body are only figures of speech, employed to help us talk about God's actions. Those mentions in Scripture of His arms, hands, eyes, and face are anthropomorphic expressions, not to be taken literally. God is a transcendent, omnipresent and immanent spirit-being. For us to see His "face" will require Him to assume a face just for our benefit; and I believe He will do just that. How will the Father's face appear? He will be the epitome of light and love, so whatever His appearance will be, seeing Him will fulfill our deepest longing. On Earth, Jesus was the visible likeness of the Father. The Bible tells us that Jesus came to show us the Father. He said, "He that has seen me has seen the Father"[10] When Jesus ascended to Heaven after the Crucifixion and the Resurrection, He ascended bodily. He took His physical body to Heaven. From that moment, there was something new in Heaven and something new in eternity. The Incarnation and Ascension events made a profound and permanent change in the Eternal Godhead! Since then, God the Son has had an added human nature and form. So, when you finally see your heavenly Father, you will look into a wonderfully familiar face. Looking into the Father's face will be like looking into the face of Jesus!

Here's something which boggles my mind. When we see Him, we will see that we have finally become like Jesus! We are told in John's first epistle, "Beloved, now we are children of God; and it has not yet been revealed what we shall be, but we know that when He is revealed, we shall be like Him, for we shall see Him as He is."[11] Not only will you look like Jesus, but you will be perfectly at home in God's family. Nothing will be strange about it! You and I have already been adopted by God into His family, as children and heirs of His eternal Kingdom. "The Spirit Himself bears witness with our spirit that we are children of God, and if children, then heirs – heirs of God and joint heirs with Christ, if indeed we suffer with Him, that we may also be glorified together."[12] On earth, a house is not a home unless family is there. It's the same in Heaven: we will feel at home because we are with family!

Almighty, awesome, and holy as He is, God has always intended to dwell with us. That's why He planted Eden in Genesis. That's why He introduced the Tabernacle to the Israelites at Mount Sinai. God wants to dwell with us. We get a sense from the prophet Jeremiah about how it will be like in that day. "No longer will a man teach his neighbor, or a man his brother, saying, 'Know the Lord,' because they will all know me, from the least of them to the greatest" (Jeremiah 31:34). No matter how unimportant and insignificant you thought you were on Earth, there you will have free access to the King of the universe. Think of it: talking and laughing with Him, eating with Him and worshiping Him. As Adam and Eve walked and talked with Him in the Garden of Eden, so will you!

What Will Our New Bodies Be Like?

"Will I be an angel?" Some people actually think that. But the Bible clearly teaches that angels are an entirely different order of wonderful created beings who are destined to serve us.[13] In Heaven you will still be a person, and you will still be human. You will still be you – without the bad parts! Moses and Elijah were still themselves when they met with Jesus on the Mount of Transfiguration.[14] Jesus said we would sit with Abraham and Isaac and Jacob – individual persons.[15] We'll all still have our personhood, complete with memory, our good character traits, gifts, passions, preferences, interests. That covers gender as well. Scripture teaches that while on earth, the distinctions between male and female disappear into the equality we all have in Christ. But that does not mean that in Heaven there will be no genders at all. In the Bible, God and Jesus are referred to with masculine pronouns. I take this to mean that gender is important in Heaven.

Your body will be physically whole and all your senses will be intact, but better than ever. Our best food here is tainted by the Curse – and our taste buds are defective as well. There's a lot about eating in scriptures about Heaven. Jesus said we would be given the fruit of the tree of life, and a new kind of manna as well. What a pity it would be if we could no longer eat when we get to Heaven! But Jesus said we shall be given the fruit to eat[16] and the manna to eat.[17] (In His resurrection body, Jesus ate fish and bread with the disciples).[18] I remember hearing, when I was a child, that when we get to Heaven we will have wonderful bodies and never need food again. I can remember thinking, childlike, "Well, then, I'm not going!" Of course we will eat in Heaven! This is the promise in Revelation 19:9, which says, "Blessed are those who are invited to the wedding supper of the Lamb!"

You will have every sensory ability that Adam and Eve had. Certainly, you will hear better and see better than you could down here. There will be warm, welcome embraces from love ones. You will enjoy hearing music in Heaven. There will be singing and great choruses of "Halleluiah" in Heaven – so of course you will have the sense of hearing. Every human ability will be enhanced in Heaven, so you should be able to hear all the sound waves including those that are now inaudible to the human ear. Another common concern for the elderly is the dimming of eyesight. In Heaven, the blind will see! According to Scripture, we see things now like seeing images in a dim mirror. [19] But there, we will see all things clearly. That tells me that our senses will be vastly improved over the abilities we have enjoyed thus far.

In Heaven, our bodies will be unburdened of the Curse which shriveled them and aged them. In Heaven we will be in a state of eternal youth. One of the concerns of growing old is the loss of energy and strength. We will have boundless energy; able to "run and not be weary!" The Bible teaches that each body will be in its glorified form.[20] That means it will be in all its God-given excellency. Our bodies will be as beautiful as those of Adam and Eve before the curse – perfect, without blemish. The Scripture teaches that we will have new powers. We are reminded by Paul in 1 Corinthians 15:43 that our body is "raised in power." Our Lord's resurrection body could go through closed doors and appear suddenly as well as disappear suddenly.[21] Jesus ascended in a physical body and defied the laws of gravity. If you say, "Well, that was Jesus and He is God," then I will say, "But Elijah was one of us, and he ascended too." The Bible says in James 5:17 that Elijah was a man with a nature like ours.

In Heaven, your body will have luminescence. The Transfiguration of Jesus, in which Moses and Elijah also appeared, gives us a hint of Heaven. When we begin to gaze upon God and Jesus in Heaven, the Holy Spirit will envelope us and transfer a shining glory to our bodies. Scripture tells us, "But we all, with unveiled face, beholding as in a mirror the glory of the Lord, are being transformed into the same image from glory to glory, just as by the Spirit of the Lord"[22] When Christ and Moses and Elijah were transfigured, they became bright like a flash of lightning[23] In other words, luminescent! Luke says Moses and Elijah appeared in "glorious splendor.[24]" This was a reference to the luminous appearance of their bodies. They were glowing with light. Stephen's face had this same glory as he looked upon the face of Jesus in Acts 6:15. According to 2 Corinthians 3:7, Moses' face had such glory on it after He saw the Lord that he had to wear a veil. Think about this: in the Bible, the only people who glowed were ones who had looked at God! God intends for you to see Him too!

From all these biblical descriptions, we know that our bodies will shine. But we won't all look the same. Different bodies will shine with distinct glories. Why will there be different glories? Perhaps because of the different kinds of sufferings and trials we have gone through in this life.[25] The apostle Paul encourages us to remember that "our light and momentary troubles are achieving for us an eternal glory that far outweighs them all."[26] Still, the appearance of your resurrection body will be recognizable. We learn from First Corinthians 13:12 that we will know as we are known. In fact, you will know everyone you meet! The disciples did not need to be told who Moses and Elijah were, although they had never met them before that moment.

Marriages Here and Relationships There

A widow who had married again once asked, "When we get to Heaven, which husband will I live with?" The answer could have been, "The one that was born again." Or the answer could have been, "We'll never know, because you are not on your way to Heaven." But the truth was that all three of them were saved. How would God work that out? Jesus was asked a similar question. The liberal Sadducees didn't believe in a resurrection, so they thought up what they believed was an absurd illustration to ridicule Jesus. They told the story of a woman who had out lived seven husbands. Whose wife was she going to be in the resurrection? Jesus, answering, said to them that the "sons of this age marry, and are given in marriage; But those who are counted worthy to attain that age, and the resurrection from the dead, neither marry, nor are given in marriage; Nor can they die any more: for they are equal unto the angels and are sons of God, being sons of the resurrection."[27]

Jesus is our authority on Heaven. He is the only one who has lived there and that has come to our planet to tell us about it. He says we will have different relationships in Heaven, and also on earth after the resurrection. We will simply be the children of God – in one great family. There will be no marriages. The need to procreate will no longer exist; for there will be no dying. We will be the products of creation by resurrection and not by natural birth. Therefore, we will also be called the "Children of the Resurrection." However, in good marriages, something deeper and more permanent develops: a true friendship which bonds the two marriage partners forever as best friends. These friendships will continue to bring joy and peace in the society of Heaven.

Looking Forward to a New Earth

Don't let all the gloom and doom predictions about the planet get you down. It will get worse before it gets better, but God hasn't given up on His plans for Earth. The present earth won't cease to be, any more than did the old earth in the days of Noah. But it will be cleansed by a world-wide fire. Peter says in 2 Peter 3:10, "But the day of the Lord will come as a thief in the night, in which the heavens will pass away with a great noise, and the elements will melt with fervent heat; both the earth and the works that are in it will be burned up." Then afterward, God will resurrect it as a glorified earth – just as He resurrects our bodies in a glorified state. The new earth will be a perfectly suitable environment in which we will dwell with God forever. He promises to bring His heavenly city down to earth and to dwell with us here on earth. Pause here and read it for yourself from your own Bible, in Revelation 21:2, 10 and 21:3.

Another description of Heaven is found in Revelation 22. It is the picture of a beautiful garden – a paradise. "Paradise" was the word which Jesus used in His promise to the dying thief. It was a Persian word which described the king's private residence: a luxurious palace surrounded by fragrant gardens of spices, exotic flowers and refreshing fountains. The beautiful new earth won't be under the curse. Try to imagine in your mind a world without the blight caused by sin's curse. Roadsides, streets, and fields will be colorfully blanketed with wonderful arrays of flowers. Gardening was Adam's first occupation in Eden, where before the curse, nothing died. Perhaps on the new Earth, there will be bountiful farmlands which will never be blighted with drought or pestilences. Gardens will abound with record-sized fruits and vegetables. The woods and fields won't have briars and thorns. Those came in with the curse and will exist no longer.

As "Tennessee Ernie" Ford used to sing, "There will be peace in the valley!" Humans won't harm other humans. Wild animals will live in harmony and will be tamely submissive to humankind. Lambs can lie down with lions. Bears will eat grass like the ox, and no animal will prey upon another. No fear of violence anywhere in the city or countryside! Rivers will be pure and uncontaminated. No trash on the highway. No dark alleys to avoid. There will be no darkness to fear. The sky will be lighted perpetually with the glory of God all over the planet, just as it was in Genesis 1:3, before the creation of the sun, the moon and the stars. No need of the sun or of the moon!

If the new Heaven is to include the continuation of Earth, the question naturally arises: "For what purpose?" The answer lies in the original purpose God had for creating Earth. God created the Earth as a place for Him to dwell with Adam and Eve. There will yet be an Earth where mankind can walk with God in holy innocence. There will yet be a time when man has stewardship and dominion over the flora and fauna of the planet. God is big enough to speak worlds and stars into space. He is certainly big enough to resurrect this planet.

Some geographical features on the planet will be changed. There won't be huge oceans, mountain ranges or deserts to limit our habitation and travel. In John's vision there was "no more sea." In Revelation 6, the mountains and islands are moved out of their places even before the planet is covered with fire. Since the curse will be removed from the earth, all the changes done to the planet as results of God's previous judgments will be undone. The ice caps created at the time of the Great Flood, as well as the mountains made by colliding continental plates and volcanic eruptions in the same geophysical cataclysm, will be gone. The huge oceans formed by the Flood will also be gone. Then, there will be ample room on the resurrected earth for a huge population of redeemed people to live in abundant prosperity.

Theologians speak of the present Heaven, where God dwells and where believers go when they die, as the "intermediate Heaven." They use that term because, according to the Bible, this is a temporary arrangement. At the end of time, God will create a new Earth. This present Earth will be "destroyed" by fire, in the same sense that it was once "destroyed" by water. There will be a new Heaven and a new Earth. God will resurrect the Earth as it was in the days of the Garden of Eden; Then He will move His dwelling place to the new Earth and dwell there with us. Since Heaven is where God is, the new Earth will then be Heaven.

Most people don't even know that God is going to transform Earth into our eternal home. But that is the promise that is repeated so often in the Bible.[28] God hasn't given up on us, and if we believe on Christ we will not only have a resurrected body, but we will one day live on a resurrected Earth. What God started in the Garden of Eden, He will one day complete on a new Earth. Read carefully the first two chapters of Genesis and then read the last two chapters of Revelation. Eden, before the fall, represents a past Earth that existed in perfection. The restored Eden in Revelation represents a future Earth that will also exist in perfection. Our present Earth is only a faint shadow land of what Earth once was. As Romans 8 tells us, it groans under the curse.[29] But there is yet to be a renewed Earth, when God has restored to its original pristine and flawless condition.

God is a creator. He is the same yesterday, today, and forever. Therefore, He continues to create. But His most magnificent creation of all will be the new Heaven and new Earth. In Isaiah 65, the prophet depicts the coming of new heavens and a new earth as God's special creation (v.17a). "So great and marvelous will this new creation be that it will erase from memory the agonies and sorrows of the old" (v. 17b).[30] "The language in Second Peter 3:13 indicates that in New Testament days the fulfillment of this prophecy was considered to lie in the future: 'Nevertheless we, according to his promise, look for new heavens and a new earth, wherein dwelleth righteousness.' The writer of Revelation also looked for the coming of a new heaven and new earth: 'And I saw a new heaven and a new earth: for the first heaven and the first earth were passed away; and there was no more sea.'"[31]

According to Revelation, there will be a great city with many gates and many streets. Nations and kings will come and go through those great gates, bringing their glory to God.[32] Such statements bring to mind the possibility of government, culture, arts and technology. Many of mankind's highest and noblest dreams were put in our hearts to be fulfilled not in this age, but in eternity! As Herbert Lockyer said it so well, "Then we shall labor for Him as we cannot now because of the trammeling influence of the flesh."[33] Think about it: even now in this life, the passion which drives you when you work at your highest aspirations makes all such work a pleasure. How much more, then will you enjoy the freedom and ability to complete all your unfinished dreams.

Getting through the traffic of the populous new Earth will present no difficulty at all. We will have a new mode of transportation. Remember how Jesus could appear suddenly in different places miles apart? Even Philip, after he baptized the Ethiopian Eunuch, was caught up by the Spirit and discovered himself 40 miles away (Acts 8:39-40). So, wherever you live on Earth, you'll only be minutes away from the City – the Heavenly Jerusalem! I think that all these things are said or hinted in Scripture in order to make us excited and expectant about Heaven. As we are told in First Corinthians 2:8-10, "Eye has not seen nor ear heard, nor have entered into the heart of man the things which God has prepared for those who love Him. But God has revealed them to us through His Spirit. For the Spirit searches all things, yes, the deep things of God."

As the preceding summary shows, God's program has been consistent from the beginning. He gave mankind a foretaste of Heaven. He created man with the power to choose, so that he might be free to reciprocate God's love. He even knew what would be man's first choice and its consequences. Yet He also knew that after seeing the terrible cost of sin, lost man would then be able to make another choice: he could choose salvation through Jesus Christ. That choice would forever settle the issue of God's goodness and secure for redeemed mankind the blessings of a perfect Earth, with God Himself dwelling with perfected mankind.

What God lays out in Genesis chapters 1-2, He finishes in the last two chapters of Revelation. Earth will be perfect again. The planet which has been corrupted by sin will be cleansed by fire. God will resurrect the Earth, just as He resurrects those who believe in Christ. Perfected people will dwell forever with God in a continuously advancing civilization on the New Earth. God, who has kept His dwelling place in what theologians call the intermediate Heaven, will bring his heavenly city, New Jerusalem, to the New Earth. The New Earth will be entirely habitable: no more seas and no more ice caps or deserts. There will be abundant room for all redeemed people from all ages to live on this planet in harmony and prosperity. The whole planet will be a delightful garden. Eden was never lost, but we were.

ENDNOTES FOR CHAPTER EIGHT

1. Paul Bilheimer, *Destined for the Throne.* (Fort Washington, Christian Literature Crusade, 1975)
2. Alcorn, 425
3. Ibid, 426
4. Hebrews 1:3
5. First Timothy 6:16b
6. Hebrews 12:14b
7. Hebrews 10:19
8. Hebrews 4:16
9. Matthew 5:8
10. John 14:9
11. First John 3:2
12. Romans 8:16-17
13. Hebrews 1:14
14. Matthew 17:3
15. Matthew 8:11
16. Revelation 2:7
17. Revelation 2:17
18. John 21:4-14
19. First Corinthians 13:12
20. First Corinthians 15:40-43
21. John 20:19 and Luke 24:31
22. Second Corinthians 3:18
23. Luke 9:29
24. Luke 9:31, NIV
25. Romans 8:17-18 and 1 Peter 5:1-4
26. Second Corinthians 4:17, NIV
27. Luke 20:34-36
28. See passages such as Isaiah 65:17; 66:22; 2 Peter 3:14; Revelation 21:1 (NKJV).
29. Romans 8:21-22
30. Gilbert L. Guffin, The Gospel in Isaiah. (Nashville: Convention Press, 1968), 126
31. Ibid.
32. Revelation 21:24-26
33. Herbert Lockyer, All the Doctrines of the Bible. (Grand Rapids: Zondervan, 1964), 289

Chapter Nine

SUDDENLY HE COMES

WE SHOULD, LIKE the biblical men of Issachar, understand the times. We have reviewed many of the signs that were predicted to precede His return, and we have shown that we live now in the season of the Second Coming. We dare not ignore such key signs as the return of Israel to its homeland, the technological revolution, world evangelization and formation of the European Union. Could other signs soon follow? In the preceding chapters we avoided dates and timetables; but repeatedly pointed to evidences of the nearness of our Lord's return. The world, as we know it, is running out of time. To use the analogy of a clock, it is shortly before midnight. The Latin expression, *ultima forsan*, meaning "it's later than you think," is sometimes inscribed on the face of a clock to indicate the idea that the time of our eternal judgment may be at hand. Not much time is left! Readiness is required. That is the point of several parables in the Gospel records.

Parables Relating to His Coming

The extended simile, or parable, was one of the favorite teaching tools of the master Teacher. Not surprisingly, many of Jesus' parables had to do with the end of the age and the time of His coming. One of the best known is the Parable of the Fig Tree, recorded in Matthew, Mark and Luke. The Luke account helps us understand that the parable was really about a characteristic of all the trees; not just a fig tree. In Luke 21:29-32, we find it stated this way:

> And He spoke to them a parable: "Look at the fig tree, and all the trees. When they are already budding, you see and know for yourselves that summer is now near. So you, likewise, when you see these things happening, know that the kingdom of God is near. Assuredly, I say to you, this generation will by no means pass away till all things are fulfilled."[1]

Many have taught and preached from this passage and told us that the fig tree is the nation Israel. While I believe that the national restoration of Israel cannot be ignored as a sign of the Lord's coming, I consider the main point of this scripture to be that the budding of the trees symbolizes the season when all the signs of the return of Jesus will be seen. The generation of which He was speaking would see all the signs fulfilled.

To faithfully teach this passage, however, we must admit to a problem with the word "generation." It seems that Jesus is saying to the disciples that their generation would not die before all the prophecy would be fulfilled and He would return. He could also have just as easily been indicating that whichever generation that would witness the beginning of this last group of signs (just mentioned in the Olivet Discourse), would see the culmination of all the signs. Understanding this statement would be less difficult for us if we all could read it in Greek. The original word used here was *genea*, which could mean a span of about 40 years; or it could mean an ethnic group. If this prediction refers to a span of 40 years, we can look to an event in A.D. 70 as the fulfillment. That would have been the destruction of Jerusalem by the Romans. But we also have to deal with the plain words of Jesus just prior to this statement. He said that we would see the Son of Man appear in the sky, and that all the tribes of the earth would mourn when they saw Him coming in the clouds.

Obviously, another meaning of the word "generation" is intended. The Jewish people, as an ethnic group, could have been intended. They would survive as a people and would not pass away until all these things had been accomplished. This promise must have been intended to prepare the Jewish believers for the massive slaughter and the destruction of their nation, just 40 years later. Throughout all the centuries from the New Testament days to modern times, the Jews have miraculously survived without a homeland. The most singular miracle of human history is the nation of Israel. Its survival and modern-day restoration to its ancient homeland is a continuing succession of miracles. Surely, the continued presence of Israel today is another proof that everything Jesus foretold will happen.

The Parable of the Ten Virgins is another appropriate reminder of our need for preparedness. There is a point in the story when the midnight cry announced the coming of the long-awaited Bridegroom. "And at midnight a cry was heard, 'Behold, the bridegroom is coming; go out to meet him!'"[2] Then there was a flurry of intense preparation. Those asleep had to be awakened. Lamps had to be trimmed. Oil had to be in adequate supply. This parable indicates what will be happening in the Church shortly before our Bridegroom comes. There will be prophetic announcements, spiritual awakening, brightening of testimonies, trimming away of fleshly hindrances, and a new demand for the oil of the Holy Spirit.

This parable refers to the whole Church, but it is also a picture of what must happen to each of us. If we are to be prepared for the Rapture, we must be like the five wise virgins; not the five foolish virgins. We must assure that we have obtained plenty of oil – a symbol of the Holy Spirit. Oil for lamps is also symbolic of preparedness for a long, patient wait. We should also awaken to greater spiritual alertness. We must act quickly to trim away our old, dead, fleshly lifestyle and allow for a brighter burning of the oil of the Holy Spirit in our hearts. Each day of our lives should be spent in eager anticipation that the return of Jesus could happen before we can lie down to sleep that night. And each night when we lie down, we should realize that we could awaken in the Rapture!

Jesus gave another parable of His coming in Luke 14. He described a great supper to which many were invited. Then at supper time, He sent his servant to announce to them, "Come, for all things are now ready."[3] In the parable, those who had already accepted invitations now began to make excuses. One was concerned about a new purchase of land; another with a new purchase of oxen; still another wanted to be excused because he was recently married. In other words, in the time since they first agreed to go to the banquet, they had become more prosperous and were preoccupied with new things and new relationships. The host was angry and immediately sent out invitations to less fortunate people, saying that none of those who were first invited would be allowed to taste the supper (even if they changed their minds). More than a powerful lesson on the principle of promise-keeping integrity, this parable points again to the need for readiness and the need to avoid preoccupying distractions. After all: if you gained the whole world, but lost your soul, it would be the biggest mistake of your lifetime! Our invitation to the Marriage Supper of the Lamb should trump all other invitations! No matter what happens, when the time comes, we should be ready to go in to the Supper!

Have you sorted this out in your thinking? Do you actually believe that Jesus could come today? At any moment we may hear the trumpet call of God, the shout of the Lord, and the voice of the archangel (First Thessalonians 4:16). When it happens, we will have no time to make further arrangements. No packing. No phone calls. No farewell notes. We will leave instantly. Jesus said, "Therefore, you also be ready, for the Son of Man is coming at an hour when you do not expect Him."[4] Jesus also posed a question: "When the Son of Man comes, will He really find faith on the earth?"[5] Faith means trusting in Christ for everything He promised, including His return. Some very sincere Christians today do not even expect Christ to return bodily. Either they have never been taught this truth from God's Word; or they have fallen away in their faith. Perhaps the secular humanist movement in public schools and universities has overwhelmed their minds with anti-supernaturalism teaching, which in itself rejects all of the biblical miracles, including the promise of the return of Christ. Have you been so influenced by anti-supernaturalism that it is difficult for you to embrace the idea of the bodily return of Jesus?

What will you be found doing when Jesus comes? What we believe shapes what we do. We cannot truly believe that Jesus is about to return if, at the same time, we are not striving to be productive and profitable for the Kingdom. If we know He is coming any day, we will consistently live to fulfill our God-given assignment on Earth. In a series of parables, Jesus taught about faithfulness in the Kingdom and how it will be rewarded when He comes again. He told the Parable of the Talents to stress the point of being useful for God (Luke 19:12-26). The nobleman gave each of his ten servants one talent (mina), which was the equivalent of about $64,000. In those days, this was a tremendous amount with which to be entrusted. The servants were to use and invest the money, and then give an accounting when the nobleman returned. After a time he returned and one servant reported that with his one mina, he had earned ten others, or $640,000. He was made ruler over ten cities. Another reported that he had earned five minas, or $320,000. He was made ruler over five cities. But one servant had not ventured to do anything at all with his mina. At least he had saved it, so he thought the nobleman would be pleased. But he was angry, and ordered the mina to be taken from him and given to the most profitable servant.

According to the verse which precedes the parable, Jesus used it to underscore that there are things which we must accomplish before His return. Each man in the parable had achieved according to his ability, except the one who did nothing. You have an assignment in life – a reason for being born. The reason still exists, or you would not have been kept alive until now by the grace of God. Your assignment is within the grasp of your ability, or it would not have been given to you in the first place. Jesus has given you something to work with, endowed you with the capacity to do it, and holds you accountable for what you do with it. When Jesus comes, will He find you occupied with the things which are related to your God-given purpose in life? It is interesting to observe what becomes important to people when they realize that they are about to go out into eternity. Things which normally consume our interest and time turn out to have no significance at all. All of us need to grasp the difference between wheat and chaff.

We should also distinguish between the wheat and the weeds in our field. One of several parables which Jesus used to refer to the end of the age was the Parable of the Wheat and Tares (Matthew 13:24-30; 36-43). The conclusion of the parable was this: the Sower was the Son of Man; the good seeds where children of the Kingdom; the weeds were sown by the devil and would be gathered at the end of the age to be burned. At the end of the age, everyone who does not belong in the Kingdom will be taken out of it; including those who practice lawlessness (as opposed to obedience). The teaching here is that if you are a child of the Kingdom, you will practice a lifestyle of obedience.

In yet another parable, Jesus said the end of the age was like a large net. In the Parable of the Large Net (Matthew 13:47-50), Jesus stressed selection and separation at the time of end. When the fish net was full, the fishermen drew it ashore and put the good fish into vessels, but tossed the bad fish away. Nothing remained in the net. The good fish went into vessels, and the bad fish were thrown away. At the end of the age, nobody is left in the net. We all have to go somewhere. The teaching point was similar to the previous parable: at the end of the age the angels would separate the wicked from the righteous. When Jesus comes, will we be found living righteously?

Yet another parable of Jesus having to do with His return, is the Parable of the Laborers (Matthew 20:1-16). It is about equal opportunities for some of us who come to work for Jesus late in the season. In this parable, seniority doesn't matter. It highlights the lateness of the time in which we serve. Some laborers were hired early in the day – about six o'clock in the morning. Some started at nine o'clock. Other groups of workers were brought in at twelve noon and at three o'clock in the afternoon. Finally, at the eleventh hour of the work day, about five o'clock in the afternoon, the last group was engaged. They had been idle all day, but came to the vineyard and joined in the work with only one hour left in the day. They received equal pay (to the chagrin of the ones who had worked through the heat of the day). The point for us is that those of us who are alive now and serving the Lord, it is like going to work in the last hour of the day.

Our reward, if we are faithful, will be the same as that of all the prophets and the apostles who have served before us. Imagine that! Think about those who have served in the heat of the day and accomplished so much more. Think what Isaiah and Paul accomplished. Think of great Christian workers like John Wesley, riding 250,000 miles on horseback throughout England, preaching 40,000 sermons, writing hundreds of books. Think what the great evangelists of the Twentieth Century accomplished: all of the great crusades of men like T. L. Osborn and Billy Graham, in which millions heard the Gospel. How could we receive an equal reward? Yet, that is the Lord's offer. It's not about merit; it's about grace. All we have to do is stop being idle and go into the vineyard!

Seeing the Second Coming in Biblical Prayers

How should the Second Coming affect your prayer life? We pray most about those things which are foremost in our heart. A good indication that you are convinced of the Lord's soon return is that the subject will come up often in your prayers. But another thing happens: you start to "see" Second Coming prayers in Bible passages. Take, for instance, the Lord's Prayer. You find more meaning in the words, "Your kingdom come, your will be done on earth as it is in heaven."[6] You comprehend what it will mean for Jesus to come and rule on this earth. You feel more like an alien in today's society. Your citizenship is in the coming kingdom. And you pray frequently and fervently for His coming.

Pray for the Righteous Judge to come. Have you slowly settled for the *status quo*? Don't give up on praying for the Lord to come and establish justice. Jesus said in Luke 18:1 that we should always pray and not give up. Then He told the parable of the persistent widow and the judge; after which, he asked, "However, when the Son of Man comes, will he find faith on the earth?"[7] From His question, it is to be inferred that when Jesus comes, He wants to find you faithfully praying and believing that God will still answer. Prayer in its most basic form is talking to God. When Jesus comes, will you still be talking to God? Or, have you already given up on praying about some things? Time has passed, and you have become discouraged. Faith has waned, and you are not praying as you should. Holding on to the hope of the Second Coming will make you like the persistent widow: you will be praying for the Judge to come and grant us justice against our adversary.

Do not forget to pray for those who face martyrdom. Did you know that souls in Heaven are praying about the persecution that is going on now? The Bible depicts people praying in the afterlife: either in Hell or in Heaven. In the Parable of the Rich Man and Lazarus, the rich man found himself in Hell and prayed that his five brothers would be warned about that horrible place.[8] In Revelation, the martyred souls under the altar are praying, "How long, Sovereign Lord, holy and true, until you judge the inhabitants of the earth and avenge our blood?"[9] More souls have been martyred for their faith in the past five decades than in all previous centuries. One of the great prayer concerns for all of us in these times ought to be intercession for the believers facing martyrdom. They are our family too. Families of victims care, and pray for justice. We have the privilege of joining our prayers to those of the martyred saints in heaven. "How long, o Lord, how long?"

Jesus told us to pray to be with Him. Even in this preliminary season before the Beginning of Sorrows and before the Tribulation, times are so tough for some in this world that they are praying for Jesus to come soon. Jesus said we should pray to escape all the things will happen in the last days. "Be always on the watch, and pray that you may be able to escape all that is about to happen, and that you may be able to stand before the Son of Man."[10] It is true that Jesus promises to always be with us, and with His presence we should fear nothing. As one country evangelist used to say, "You should be ready to swing out over Hell on a rotten corn stalk and sing 'Amazing Grace!'" But God is merciful, and Jesus Himself encourages us to pray to escape the worst days this planet will ever see.

Pray for one another to be more completely sanctified before Jesus comes. That's the prayer with which Paul closes his first letter to the Thessalonians. He said, "Now may the God of peace Himself sanctify you completely; and may your whole spirit, soul, and body be preserved blameless at the coming of our Lord Jesus Christ."[11] You may have friends who are praying that prayer for you right now. Nothing more wonderful can happen to you in this life than for intercessors to pray for your sanctification. That means that they are praying that you will separate yourself from unholy things; that you will give yourself to God in every way; and that you will be found blameless at the coming of Christ. And when you pray that prayer for others, you become their best friend!

The last prayer in the Bible is for Jesus to come! John, at the close of the Book of Revelation, is responding to the thrice-repeated promise by Jesus that He is coming quickly. John prays, "Even so, come, Lord Jesus!" When you pray that simple prayer, you are getting with God's program; lining up with all the prophets, apostles, and angels of Heaven. You're praying for the Kingdom to come; for the earth to be full of the knowledge of the Lord; for the Devil and Antichrist to be thrown into the lake of fire. If you pray that prayer aloud in the company of others, you can get the attention of lost people, worry carnal Christians, and scare demons! More importantly, praying for Jesus to come will set your mind on heavenly things and help you let go of worldly ambitions. When you say, "Even so, come, Lord Jesus!" you are praying to see Jesus in all His glory as King of Kings and Lord of Lords! When the Second Coming becomes a personal passion, you will pray more powerfully.

An Atomic Moment

What on Earth will happen when the Bible's last prayer is finally fulfilled? What will it be like on this planet when the Rapture suddenly comes? Can you imagine seeing someone just dematerialize in front of you, without your eyes even having time to blink? That's what the sudden disappearance of believers will be like for those who are left behind. That's the way it happened in the translation of Enoch in Genesis 5 (also mentioned in Hebrews 11:5). He "was;"

then suddenly, "was not!" The Greek New Testament describes the moment of the Rapture in First Corinthians 15:52 with the word *atomos* plus the prefix *alpha*. Our English word "atom" comes from *atomos*, which itself comes from the Greek root "temno" (to cut). The word "moment" here means "that which cannot be cut into or divided." The idea is that our change will take place in an instant of time so small that it cannot be divided: an atomic moment! To the Greek mind, the moment was the smallest unit of time, indivisible. There are said to be 25 "moments" in the "twinkling of an eye." The believers who are living at the time when Jesus returns will be snatched from the earth and transformed into glorified bodies in a moment far quicker than the blinking of an eye!

Even so, according to First Thessalonians 4, the believers who are alive will not precede those who have already died. They will rise first! Even though the atomic moment of the Rapture is quicker than the blink of an eye, the first event during that moment will be the resurrection and glorification of those who have died in Christ. We, who have mourned the loss of loved ones through the years, are to be comforted with the thought that Jesus will bring them all with Him when He comes. They and all the saints of all the centuries before will appear in glorified bodies and fill the air around Jesus. We who are alive and remain will be caught up in the same moment, to be with them and to be with Jesus. Paul assures us that, from that point forward, we will be with the Lord forever! Whatever happens on Earth; we will be safely with Jesus. How quickly our situation will change! Be comforted with this thought when you are passing through tough times. Any day now, it can happen. The last three sayings of Jesus are recorded in Revelation 22. He says three times, "I come quickly!" When He comes quickly, we will go quickly.

Suddenly: not here, but there! Like Enoch, we will be translated. Translated into a spiritual dimension that is so close to us it is nearer than our next breath, and at the same time is as physically far removed from us as the "third heaven." In the ancient mindset, there were three heavens. The first heaven was the cloudy atmosphere. The second heaven was the firmament of the stars. The third heaven was far beyond the stars. Even the distance to stars is so great that it must be measured in light years. Light travels at the speed of 186,000 feet per second. It has taken the light of some of the stars 500,000,000 years to reach Earth. If in the Rapture we traveled from Earth as slowly as the speed of light, we would require at least 500,000,000 years to reach Heaven, and perhaps many more. But we will go to Heaven in an atomic moment, faster than the speed of thought. One moment on earth, the next moment in Heaven! What a blessed moment!

Entering Eternity

Entering eternity as a born-again child of God holds no real fear. We often hear it mentioned that the only fear for a Christian facing death is a fear of the "unknown." Yet when we fully understand the plain teaching of Scripture, there is much to anticipate that will be not be unknown, but very familiar. In Chapter Eight, we revisited the numerous scriptures about Heaven and found that Heaven is designed to make us feel at home. There are three great reasons that you will feel right at home. First of all, you really shouldn't feel at all strange in the presence of the awesome Godhead. We already know Jesus. We know Him well from the Gospel stories and from living with His spirit inside us. And because He came to show us the Father and to baptize us with the Holy Spirit, we already know so much about our Heavenly Father and the Holy Spirit that we will feel as if we have come home to our real family.

Secondly, Heaven will be populated with so many people we have known on earth, it will be like going back to our hometown. We will see all of our family members who died in Christ: our children, parents, grandparents, brothers, sisters, aunts, uncles, and cousins. We will see classmates and old friends. There will be believers we knew in our places of employment. A special joy will be to see all those whom we have introduced to Christ through our personal witness. Think about meeting again with all the fellow church members whom we have known over the years of our lives on earth! They will look better than the last time you saw them. And this time when they tell you, "You're looking good," you can believe them. All the saints of church history, whose life stories we have studied, will be there for us to meet. From the Bible, we will be well-acquainted with such wonderful old friends as Abraham, Moses, David, Peter, John and Paul. Heaven will be the greatest reunion you could ever imagine! Everywhere you turn, you will see people that you know.

But there is a third reason Heaven will be very familiar to you. We shared in the preceding chapter how God is going to resurrect the earth itself for our eternal home. He promises in His word to make it all new and perfect. This time, Eden-like conditions will prevail all over the planet. God says in Isaiah 65: 17, "For behold, I create new heavens and a new earth, and the former shall not be remembered or come to mind." Again, He tells us in Isaiah 66:22, "For as the new heavens and the new earth which I will make shall remain before me, says the Lord…" In the New Testament, He tells us through the words of Peter in Second Peter 3:13, "Nevertheless we, according to His promise, look for new heavens and a new earth in which righteousness dwells." John speaks in Revelation 21:1 of seeing "a new heaven and a new earth, for the first heaven and first earth had passed away…" But the point is this: the earth will still be in many ways the same earth. Having a resurrected earth on which to live is like having a resurrected body. Neither will be unfamiliar to you! Just as you know and are familiar with the parts of your own body, you will also be familiar with the new earth.

No Other Way

Seeing the signs is both heartwarming and heart-wrenching. The heart-wrenching part is in knowing that many friends and loved ones are not ready for His coming. An old evangelist used to say, "Anybody, even with no more sense God gave to a billy goat, would want to go to Heaven!" So it would seem. Yet, Heaven is a prepared place for a prepared people. Jesus, and only Jesus, can prepare us for Heaven. There is no other way to Heaven. Some falsely assume that because God is so good, and because they themselves are not so bad, they will automatically be received in Heaven when they die. Of course in their sin-darkened minds they have no idea of how unholy they are when compared to God. And they show themselves ignorant of the main message of God's Word.

What can you do for someone who may miss Heaven? First of all, pray earnestly for them to know the truth. Here's the truth that they need to know: to get to Heaven, every soul must come to God in the same way. God loved us so much that He gave His only son to die for us. And Jesus loves us so much that He even prayed for us while we were killing Him. Jesus said that we must be born again. He taught that in order to do this, we must repent for our sinfulness and receive Him as Savior. There are two words associated in the New Testament with the idea of salvation. The words are "repent" and "believe." The word for repent is *metanoeo*; and refers to a change of mind that results in turning from sin and turning to Christ. The word for believe in the New Testament is *pisteuo*, which means to trust in, cling to, rely upon. It indicates a continuing, intimate relationship of loving, obedient, trusting in Jesus. When you pray for lost friends, pray that they learn biblical truths about salvation.

What about God's goodness? Surely, God would not let your friends go to such an awful place as Hell? Here's the deal: God sent His Son precisely because He did not want your friends to go to Hell. Living their lives at a distance from Jesus will forever distance them from their only hope of Heaven. Certainly, God is good! But for us to ignore His goodness all our lives; yet believe somehow that we can trust in God's goodness when we die, is to live in arrogant foolishness. Here is what the Scripture says in First John 5:11-12. "And this is the testimony: that God has given us eternal life, and this life is in His Son. He who has the Son has life; he who does not have the Son of God does not have life." God's goodness can be expressed in no greater way.

You have a friend who tells you that he is already a good person? That would be great, if only it were true. But it still wouldn't get him into Heaven. Jesus said that no one comes to the Father except by Him.[12] No matter how good we think we are, the Bible says all have sinned, and the wages of sin is death.[13] The problem with our goodness is that we are usually comparing ourselves with other human beings. There are some really wicked people on this earth, and they make us look good by comparison. But none of us are righteous enough to get into Heaven. To get an idea of how sinful we are, we need only to take a good look at God's "Top Ten." The rich young ruler in Luke 18 thought he had kept the Ten Commandments from his youth up. But when Jesus tested him on the very first one, he found he had failed. The laws of God do not save us, anyway. They just prove that we need God's mercy through Jesus.

The bottom line is this: there's no other way to Heaven. Someone has said that the distance between Hell and Heaven is about eleven inches. That is the approximate distance between the brain and the heart. Our head sometimes hinders our hearts from opening up to Jesus. Yet, Jesus loves us so much that if we do repent and humble ourselves as little children, He will in no way refuse to save us. You should earnestly pray that, somehow, your friend's heart will open up and receive the truth – whatever it takes! However, you should know one important thing. When you pray, "whatever it takes," you are making yourself available as well. Besides praying for that person, you must be ready to say something. Think about how wonderful it was that someone got your attention about Jesus! Don't neglect your God-given opportunities to turn the attention of friends and loved ones toward Jesus. This includes your Christian friends who may be living beneath their privileges.

A Blessed Assurance

"I hope so!" That was the answer that perplexed me many years ago when I asked veteran saints if they knew for sure they were going to Heaven. The previous generation of the church did not take eternity lightly. In the early years of ministry, I met many who had served and honored Jesus faithfully for fifty or sixty years. I expected to hear them answer, "Yes." Perhaps because of the abundance of "hell, fire and damnation" sermons in those days, they weren't quite sure if they had been "faithful enough." The main problem for them, and perhaps for you, is an understanding of who does the saving. We will never get to Heaven by being faithful enough. No measuring device exists which can quantify your goodness or faithfulness in order to determine if you qualify for Heaven. How then can you be sure?

Maybe I should have led with a different question when I spoke with that older generation. Maybe I should have asked, "Do you enjoy Jesus?" Whoever truly enjoys an inward presence of Jesus now, and continues to do so, can be confident about Heaven. If I understand correctly, my assurance of salvation does not rest upon a decision which I made years ago. It rests upon the relationship which has resulted from that decision. Do I enjoy Jesus in my life now? My answer is, "Yes!" When I was very young, I broke the law and went to jail. But I made a decision there in that jail to repent and receive Jesus as my Saviour. That decision began a conscious relationship which has lasted more than 51 years now. In humble prayer, I confessed that I was a lost sinner and that my only hope was for Jesus to forgive me and save me. I gave my whole life to Him; inviting Him to be my Lord. He forgave me and began to show me how to walk with Him. Now, I simply enjoy Jesus in daily life.

Let me explain what I mean by "enjoying Jesus." From that first moment in the jail to this very day, I'm still learning how to walk more closely to Jesus. He's been my Faithful Friend who always picked me up when I stumbled; always embraced me again when I wandered away. He's the Center in the very core of my Being who keeps me warm inside. I can not even imagine the cold, empty loneliness of His absence. There have been some surprises along the way, however. Loving Him has drawn me, sometimes a bit unwillingly, into loving others who love Him. I found that I could not follow Him unless I also loved His Church. He's coming back for the Church, which is portrayed as His Bride. Loving Him has also caused me to forgive some folk I didn't plan on forgiving. And loving Him has led me to seek forgiveness from others. My real joy and peace in life come from a simple willingness to do things His way.

The Billy Graham crusades helped make the popular hymn, "Blessed Assurance," even more famous. Its words were written by a blind composer, Fanny Crosby (1820-1915). Her heart was full of anticipation of the coming of the Lord. The three stanzas printed below reflect Fanny's deep love of Jesus and her hope of the Rapture:

> Blessed assurance, Jesus is mine! O what a foretaste of glory divine! Heir of salvation, purchase of God, born of His Spirit, washed in His blood.
>
> Perfect submission, perfect delight! Visions of rapture now burst on my sight; angels descending bring from above echoes of mercy, whispers of love.
>
> Perfect submission – all is at rest, I in my Savior am happy and blessed; watching and waiting, looking above, filled with His goodness, lost in His love.[14]

The refrain which follows each stanza is a chorus which should resonate in the heart of every believer in these times when His coming seems so near:

> *This is my story, this is my song, praising my Savior all the day long; this is my story, this is my song, praising my Savior all the day long.*[15]

ENDNOTES FOR CHAPTER NINE

---

1. Luke 21:29-32
2. Matthew 25:6
3. Luke 14:17b
4. Matthew 24:44
5. Luke 18:8
6. Matthew 6:10, NIV
7. Luke 18:8b, NIV
8. Luke 16:27
9. Revelation 6:10, NIV
10. Luke 21:36, NIV
11. First Thessalonians 5:23
12. John 14:6
13. Romans 3:19-23 and Romans 6:23
14. Robert K. Brown and Mark R. Norton, *Great Songs of Faith.* (Carol Stream, IL: Tyndale House Publishers, 1995), 128
15. Ibid.

Bilheimer, Paul. *Destined for the Throne.* Fort Washington, Christian Literature Crusade, 1975.

Brown, Robert K. and Mark R. Norton. *Great Songs of Faith.* Carol Stream, IL: Tyndale House Publishers, 1995.

Buckingham, Jamie., in *The Rapture Book* by Doug Chatham. Monroeville, PA: Whitaker House, 1974.

Ehrlich,Eugene. *Amo, Amas, Amat and More.* NY: Harper & Row, 1985.

Fedler, Jon. "Israel's Agriculture in the 21st Century." http://www.mfa.gov.il/MFA/Facts, Nov. 11, 2008.

Felter, Nurit. "Israel to Export 125 Million Flowers to Europe." http:www.ynetnews.com/articles, Jan. 31, 2007.

Charles H. Dyer. *World News and Bible Prophecy.* Wheaton, IL: Tyndale House, 1993.

Guffin, Gilbert L. *The Gospel in Isaiah.* Nashville: Convention Press, 1968.

Halley Henry H. *Halley's Bible Handbook.* Grand Rapids: Zondervan, 1965.

Havner, Vance. *In Times Like These.* Old Tappan, NJ: Fleming H. Revell Co., 1969.

Lockyer, Herbert. *All the Doctrines of the Bible.* Grand Rapids: Zondervan, 1964.

Long, Justin. "Least-Reached Peoples," *Mission Frontiers* May-June 2006

Lowell, James Russell., in *Bartlett's Familiar Quotations,* 15th ed. Boston: Little, Brown and Co., 1980

May, Neal W. *Israel a Biblical Tour of the Holy Land.* Tulsa: Albury Publishing, 2000. *Quran, The Holy*: Surah 2:66, Surah 5:60 and Surah 7:166.

Ryken, Leland, James C. Wilhoit, Tremper Longman III, eds. *Dictionary of Biblical Imagery*. Downers Grove, IL: InterVarsity Press, 1998

Sabine Baring-Gould, "Onward Christian Soldiers," in *The Baptist Hymnal.* Nashville, Convention Press, 1956.

Sachar, Howard M. *A History of Israel from the Rise of Zionism to Our Time*. New York: Alfred A. Knopf, Inc., 1996.

Slade, Mary B. C. "The Kingdom Is Coming," in *The Baptist Hymnal.* Nashville: Convention Press, 1956.

Smolin, Lee. *The Trouble With Physics*. NY: Houghton Mifflin Company, 2006.

Tapia, Andres. "Is World Ripe For Revival?" <u>Christianity Today</u> November 14, 1994; December 22, 2008.

Tenney, Merrill C., Ed. *Zondervan Pictorial Bible Dictionary.* Grand Rapids: Zondervan, 1963.

Walter, Walker. *Extraordinary Encounters With God.* (Ann Arbor: Servant Publications, 1997.

Walvoord, John F. *The Revelation of Jesus Christ*. Chicago: Moody Press, 1966.

Notes

Notes